Duvel
à la carte

CONTENTS

07 DUVEL'S DUEL
A world-famous beer meets world-famous chefs

09 THE LIFE HISTORY OF DUVEL

17 PREFACE MICHEL MOORTGAT

18 PREFACE PIERRE WYNANTS (B)
Grilled medallions of rabbit fillet with Duvel and Namur snails

22 JONNIE BOER, DE LIBRIJE (NL)
Hot langoustines with spaghetti, paprika
   and sabayon of Duvel with a mature farmhouse cheese
Tartare of langoustines with beetroot and Duvel tea
Cabbage-fed hare with Münster cheese, kale
   and sauce royale enriched with Duvel
Epoisses crème brulée, fennel sorbet

38 WOUT BRU, BISTROT D'EYGALIÈRES (F)
Raw scallops with goose liver,
   Duvel vinaigrette
Fritters with Duvel and petits gris snails, paprika coulis with ginger
Perch fillet poached in Duvel consommé

54 RUDY BUCHET,
AU SANGLIER DES ARDENNES (B)
Fillet of wild duck with 'aigrelette' sauce, sauerkraut with Duvel
Casserole of wild rabbit with Duvel

62 CHRISTIAN DENIS, CLOS ST. DENIS (B)
Supreme of goose- and duck livers with spice cake
   and Vrolingen syrup, chutney of conference pears
   with Duvel beer

Duvel
à la carte

Stefaan Daeninck
Sven Everaert

lannoo

Tatin of chicory with acacia honey, fried turbot
   and a reduction of Duvel beer
Caramelized puff pastry with apples, sorbet of Duvel beer

76 WILLIAM DRABBLE, AUBERGINE (GB)
Glazed belly of pork with cabbage, potatoes with Duvel infusion
Mullet escabeche with Duvel

86 PETER GOOSSENS, HOF VAN CLEVE (B)
Fried sole with oxheart cabbage and mussels, Duvel sabayon
Casserole of pig's cheek with Duvel and croquettes of sweetcorn
Salad of prawns, avocado and Duvel sorbet

100 SERGIO HERMAN, OUD SLUIS (NL)
Grilled turbot with fried Zeeland lobster, cream of Jerusalem artichokes
   and lobster sauce with Duvel and spices
Three coffee structures, with a sabayon of chocolate and Duvel

112 EDDY KERKHOFS, IL PICCOLINO (USA)
Shoulder of lamb à la Tante Marie,
   or Shoulder of lamb with Duvel
Three times crab with Duvel sauce

122 MANUEL MARTINEZ, LE RELAIS LOUIS XIII (F)
Fried turbot, poultry gravy with Duvel foam
Oxtail with black truffle and Duvel

136 JACQUES & LAURENT POURCEL, LE JARDIN DES SENS (F)
Stuffed fillet of rabbit, preserved rabbit legs with Duvel and sweet onion, Duvel emulsion

146 JACQUES & LAURENT POURCEL AND CHRISTOPHE LANGRÉE, W' SENS (GB)
Braised cod fillet, potato ragout,
   bouchot mussels and Duvel
Casserole of pig's cheeks with Duvel

Duvel's Duel
a world-famous beer meets world-famous chefs

How can a leading international beer be honourably put in the limelight other than by the hand of the master himself? The master, the leading international chef, is obviously the right person to highlight the unique nature of Duvel in a concoction specially created for it.

In this confrontation we follow Duvel across national frontiers: from Belgium, via our neighbours, the Netherlands, France and the United Kingdom, to the United States.

Two champions fight a duel, with on one side Duvel, and on the other the master chef who has already seen his capabilities crowned by Michelin stars. And the main issue? To move the frontiers. To put the spotlight on special features. To conjure with tastes. A confrontation with their own personalities.

As a chef I work in my development and creative enterprise, Culinair Ateljee, every day thinking up recipes and creating striking dishes. But for this occasion I was able to hang up my apron. For once, I could put each master chef through the mill myself. I could observe and record, niggle at their innermost feelings and invade their nerve centre, their kitchen. Besides, I could not settle for the commonplace. We all know that these starred chefs have a sixth sense enabling them to spot the best ingredients and to combine and present them in perfect proportions. That they are perfectionists, workaholics and ambitious, seems obvious. We would like to know more. What is this man like when he takes off his chef's hat? As a father, a husband, as a personality? His vocation, his passions, particularly as they affect Duvel, that is what fascinates us. In all this I had to be the observer. What an honour!

It would not be a simple job. But I assumed that the fact that I am a chef myself would clear the way for me.

For the finishing touch we had to find the right photographer. And as culinary creativity and ambience play an equally important part in this book, the right photographer had to be someone who had already earned his stripes in both fields. In other words, it would have to be Sven Everaert!

Finally a piece of good advice – learnt from experience. Before you enthusiastically start reading or cooking, treat yourself to the creator of the right atmosphere, and enjoy a Duvel!
Cheers!,

Stefaan Daeninck

The first Belgian brewery with an HACCP certificate

In 2001 Duvel Moortgat obtained the much coveted HACCP certificate, a quality label for the manufacture and conditioning of beers. It is the ultimate crown for their consistent quality control during and after the complete production process, the strictest possible monitoring of the supply of raw materials and their precise origin. Duvel Moortgat is in fact the first Belgian brewery to be awarded this prestigious certificate.

The life history of Duvel

The Duvel Moortgat brewery can look back with pride on a rich history of more than 130 years of passionate and professional skills in brewing. It all began with Jan-Leonard Moortgat, ancestor and founder, who with his wife Maria De Block founded the Moortgat farm brewery in 1871. Nothing remarkable so far; there were a good 3,000 breweries operating in Belgium around the turn of the century.

Jan-Leonard experimented by trial and error and wrestled his way brilliantly through the difficult early years. His high-yeast beers were soon highly regarded in Puurs and its surroundings and soon also became popular among the citizens of Brussels. He opened a depot in Laken, the start of an unstoppable success story. The second generation, too, caught the beer virus, and his sons Albert and Victor went into the business: Albert as the brewer, while Victor looked after sales, in the 1920s still delivering by horse and cart. There was a real break-through in the aftermath of the First World War, when Belgium was in close contact with the United Kingdom and its popular ales. This made Albert decide to design a beer on the British model. For this he had to get hold of a sample of local yeast, so he set course for Scotland. After a little while, and with the necessary powers of persuasion, he was able to obtain the much coveted yeast sample from the Scottish brewers. It is interesting to know that the brewery today still uses yeast grown from that original Scottish strain, which contributed to an important extent to the high quality and special taste of the beer. Back in Belgium Albert set himself to brewing, which resulted in a new, magnificent beer with which the brewery would make history. With the end of the First World War in mind, he christened this special brew 'Victory Ale'… Not for long, it turned out! On tasting it, a friend described the brew as 'the very Devil'. This closed the circle for the Moortgat brothers: from 1923 onwards the new 'divine' beer was marketed under the name 'Duvel' – and that, of course, translates as 'Devil' in English. Catholic Flanders was a little shocked by the name, but after tasting it, quickly threw all scruples overboard.

From the 1950s onwards the third generation also worked in the family business and the brewery was developed further technically and commercially. The international break-through came in the 1970s.

By 1999 what had once started as a small-scale, traditional family farm brewery had grown into one of the most important Belgian brewery groups. Export successes piled up abroad. To encourage further growth and to ensure continuity the fourth generation of Moortgats decided in 1999 to launch it on the stock exchange, at the same time changing the name to Duvel Moortgat.

Duvel Moortgat shifts its beer frontiers

In recent years Duvel Moortgat has known increasing international success resulting particularly from the increasing export of its own Belgian beers, as well as from the production of local beers in its establishments abroad.

That the Czech Republic, the nursery of pils and the country with the largest consumption of beer per head of population, had a role to play in the internationalization of Duvel Moortgat was obvious. Since 2001 Duvel Moortgat has held 50 % of the shares in the Czech Bernard brewery which in that country plays an important role in the field of premium pils beers.

Barely two years later, in 2003, Duvel Moortgat took over the American 'Brewery Ommegang' to brew local special craft beers in authentic Belgian style. The main brands of this brewery are 'Ommegang', the wheat beer 'Ommegang Witte', 'Hennepin', 'Rare Vos' and 'Three Philosophers'. Each of them high-yeast beers, with a second fermentation in bottle, typical of Duvel Moortgat. Moreover, in the brewing process they make use of Belgian malt and the same kinds of hops, Saaz and Styria, that are also found in Belgian beer.

Duvel, the showpiece

Not for nothing has Duvel Moortgat gained recognition round the world as the international standard in the field of blonde high-yeast beers, with a second fermentation in bottle. This dominant position is without doubt due to its champion beer, Duvel, which today enjoys extraordinary popularity in all parts of the world.

Whereas in 1926 the annual production of Duvel amounted to 300 crates a year, the brewery currently achieves an annual production of a good 80 million bottles, of which more than 20 per cent is destined for export. In Belgium Duvel is the best-selling special beer with a second fermentation in bottle. For more than ten years sales have risen uninterruptedly in Belgium and in the important export markets: the Netherlands, France, The United Kingdom and the United States.

Savoir vivre: beer and the ritual of pouring

What makes Duvel so special is the maturing process of two months in warm and cold cellars. The cold 'lagering', after a second fermentation in bottle in the warm cellar, is in fact a unique process in the world. The beer owes its sophisticated taste and aroma to an important degree to this process.

Duvel's light, fruity, dry aroma results in part from the use of the finest hops. These types of hops, combined with the yeast used, are largely behind the secret of Duvel's subtle, bitter strength.

A Duvel is best served in its typical tasting glass. Of course, you make sure that the glass is clean and dry. Then hold the glass at an angle and let the beer slide slowly and close to the rim to the bottom. Avoid any contact between the glass and the bottle. Halfway through pouring, bring the glass slowly upright and you can then steadily pour the rest.

Be sure to leave one centimetre with the yeast in it in the bottle. These dregs are perfectly healthy and good for the digestion, but they give the beer a bitter taste and cloudy look when it is poured out. Make it a rule to store the bottles upright to keep the dregs at the bottom, ready for pouring. To enjoy the taste of Duvel at its best we recommend serving it cool at 6 °C - 7 °C.

Thanks to its authentic brewing process with a yeast which is actually still cultivated on the basis of the original 1918 Scottish strain, Duvel is a completely pure and natural product. The beer has an alcohol content of 8.5% vol., is fat free and contains only 198 k/calories per bottle. As a result of the second fermentation in bottle the beer can be kept for at least three years in optimal conditions, such as a cool dark place. After that the beer will still be drinkable, but the taste evolves, becoming heavier and sweeter, like an old port.

Its dry and yet lightly alcoholic-sweet taste makes Duvel a pleasant beer that will not let itself be pushed into a corner. Duvel provides a thirst-quenching drink on every occasion, from an aperitif to a digestif. Duvel is both a unique beer for drinking on its own, and the ideal accompaniment for many snacks and dishes. But on top of that, it is a valuable ingredient in the kitchen, giving a dish additional taste values. Simple cooking or an exquisite cuisine, Duvel improves both. In this book the master chefs want to convince every Duvel lover to work creatively with this beer. You will have all the credit of impressing yourself and your guests.

A unique tasting glass

A unique beer requires a unique tasting glass to maximize the perception of it. In the late 1960s the brewery designed the perfect glass. In doing so they took account of a number of criteria. The first requirement is the size. A glass had to be developed that makes it possible to pour out the whole of a 33 cl bottle. Second requirement, the shape! Only a round tulip shape makes it possible to experience to the full the heavenly taste and aroma of a Duvel. Because the glass tapers slightly towards the top, the aeration is retained as much as possible. So the glass contributes among other things to maintaining the head of froth. In this special glass, drink and head are perfectly in balance, whereas a classic glass will cause an explosion of froth when it is poured out.

A Duvel is not perfect without its typical bubbles, which in their turn help to maintain the head. This bubbling is among other things caused by etching in the bottom of the bowl. In the 'old' glasses this etching consisted of a little scratch, in the current glasses it is a D, the first letter of the Duvel logo.

To protect the beer from sunlight, and so to guarantee its unique taste, Duvel is bottled in robust, brown, round bottles.

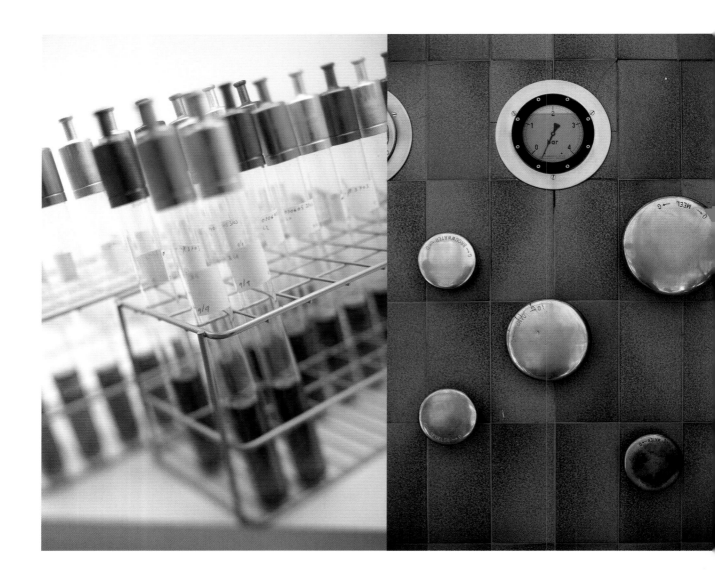

The abbey beers of Maredsous

Since 1963 the Abbey of Maredsous has entrusted the
brewing of its Maredsous beers to the Duvel Moortgat brewery.
Under the strict supervision of the fathers from the Benedictine
abbey, Duvel Moortgat has since then brewed their blonde
beer with an alcohol content of 6% vol., the brown variant with
an alcohol content of 8% vol., and the triple with an alcohol
content of 10% vol. The beers are first matured for two full
months before setting out for their final destinations. The
specific second fermentation in the bottle, perfected by the
brewery for their main brand, Duvel, gives an extra dimension
to the Maredsous abbey beers too. Whichever colour or taste
you prefer, the Maredsous range has everything to tempt
you. The blonde Maredsous combines various varieties of
malt and hops, resulting in a harmonious taste experience.
A touch of fruitiness enriches the predominantly fresh, slightly
bitter aftertaste. The brown Maredsous hides under its deep
brown Burgundy colour a very expressive palette of aromas.
A generous caramel bouquet is perfectly supplemented by
masterly measured touches of fruit. The deep-blonde coloured
Maredsous triple is known for its very fine sparkle. Sour, sweet
and bitter merge perfectly together in a clean, full taste with
a heart-warming aftertaste. The rich and unique taste of the
Maredsous abbey beers makes each of them a welcome
ingredient in the kitchen too.

Vedett

Other established values of the Duvel Moortgat brewery are
their premium beers, Vedett and Bel Pils.
Vedett, with an alcohol content of 5% vol., is currently the fashionable beer and the brewery's most individual brew. Its image
is hip, young, innovative and a little absurd.
Vedett started its career a good half century ago as one of
many 'export beers'. Although originally Vedett enjoyed mainly
local popularity in the Antwerp-Brussels region, many catering
establishments have meanwhile discovered its qualities.

Bel Pils

Bel Pils, Duvel Moortgat's luxury pils beer with an alcohol content of 5.2% vol., was created in 1930 as 'Extra Blond'. Over the years the name changed several times, as in 'Dubbel Blond' (and 'Extra Pilsner'). Today we know it as 'Bel Pils'. This beer is one of the most authentic and traditional Belgian low-fermentation luxury pils beers. Despite its many name changes the original recipe and ingredients have always been respected and still are. Its unique bitter and typical taste is obtained by using the finest Saaz hops. The special lager yeast ensures that the taste of Bel Pils is much more aromatic than other pils beers. With its mildly sweet, fruity and hoppy touches of taste it is the thirst quencher par excellence.

Steendonk

In 1989 another joint working agreement was clinched with the Palm brewery. The result is a cloudy, lightly hopped and high-quality wheat beer with an alcohol content of 4.5% vol., called Steendonk. The name is a combination of Steenhuffel and Breendonk, the two districts where the Palm and Duvel Moortgat breweries are located. This tasty thirst quencher derives its typical taste from its special combination of malted barley, unmalted wheat, coriander and curaçao. Its taste and aroma are further refined by the soecial process of a second fermentation.

15

'We are at the moment in the middle of a gastronomic revolution. In New York and Paris, as well as in Amsterdam and London.'

One of the new trendsetters is undoubtedly cooking with beer. Beer accompanies more and more dishes. With its rich palette of tastes and aromas Duvel lends itself as an outstanding ingredient to add a distinctive accent to many culinary specialities. In this book a number of chefs with an international reputation illustrate how Duvel fits perfectly into the leading cuisines of the world.

At the highest level there are a number of common factors in beer brewing and gastronomy! For both, only the best raw materials or ingredients are good enough. Both require a well-thought-out technique and of course a large dose of dedication. Only after all these factors have been satisfied to the full can we expect the best results.
For years the Duvel Moortgat brewery has imposed the highest demands upon itself. To start with there is the delicate choice of the right raw materials which we need as brewers. In addition we have to apply the most innovative technologies. But at the same time we must always bear in mind that the end result, the sublime taste of Duvel, must remain the same. The common grounds with a master chef are legion. He, too, must innovate and be conversant with the latest techniques, but must always stay true to his starting point, his ingredients and the pursuit of the most delicious and balanced end result.

So I would like to put on record my deep respect for the chefs and extend my thanks to them for taking part. They show that with Duvel as an ingredient, or as a drink to accompany the dish, magnificent results can be achieved.

Every self-respecting restaurant today has a comprehensive wine list. Why not introduce a selective beer list, to which an extensive palette of tastes can be matched. Beer in no way needs to be inferior to wine.
With this splendid book, with its pictures, text and recipes, Duvel Moortgat wants to put an end to this misapprehension once and for all. The dishes, specially developed here with Duvel as an ingredient, or as a drink to accompany them, should convince any non-believers!

Michel Moortgat
CEO Duvel Moortgat

Pierre Wynants
Comme chez Soi
Brussels (B)

'Every chef swears allegiance to the use of high-quality ingredients in his kitchen. My son-in-law, Lionel, and I are enormously proud of being able to boast of a wealth of Belgian regional products. Right from the first day that Comme chez Soi opened, we have lovingly used them in our dishes. Some of them have a world-wide reputation: think of our chocolates, hops, chicory, asparagus, North Sea prawns… and of course our delicious beers. It is a great honour for me to be able to come forward as ambassador of a special beer such as Duvel. We Belgians can surely be a little bit chauvinist about it: beer is for Belgium what wine is for France.

A beer such as Duvel deserves to be put on a pedestal and while you are doing that, make sure it is made of the most expensive marble! Whether as an ingredient in a dish or as the drink to accompany it, Duvel is always the perfect partner.

For these reasons I applaud initiatives such as this splendid book. And I am not alone in this, as can be seen from the enthusiasm with which my colleagues have extended their culinary cooperation.

Enjoy cooking, reading and leafing through this book!
Pierre Wynants

Grilled medallions
of rabbit fillet with Duvel
and Namur snails

INGREDIENTS

For the snails and the sauce :
- *40 g large mushrooms*
- *40 g artichoke hearts, cooked*
- *40 g tomato, skinned and without seeds*
- *80 g butter*
- *20 snails 'petits gris de Namur'*
  in their cooking liquid
- *15 g shallots, finely chopped*
- *4 cl Duvel*
- *8 cl poultry stock*
- *8 cl cooking liquid from the snails*
- *freshly ground pepper and sea salt*

For the tabouleh :
- *200 g semolina (tabouleh),*
  steeped in poultry stock
- *60 g young carrots,*
  cooked and cut into cubes
- *60 g French beans,*
  cooked and cut into cubes
- *30 g spring onion, finely chopped*
- *40 g red paprika,*
  skinned and cut into cubes
- *10 cl olive oil*
- *freshly ground pepper and sea salt*

For the rabbit fillets :
- *2 rabbit fillets, without membranes*
- *leaves of fresh thyme*
- *peanut oil*
- *freshly ground pepper and sea salt*

For the garnish :
- *6 g parsley leaves*
- *4 g sprigs of dill*

PREPARATION

The sauce and the snails
Cut the mushrooms, the artichoke hearts and the tomato into 0.8 cm cubes.
Melt 40 g butter and brown the snails in it. Season to taste with pepper and salt.
Take the snails out of the pan and put them to one side. Put the mushrooms and the artichoke cubes in the pan.
Add the shallots. Braise for another 2 minutes and deglaze with the Duvel, the cooking liquid from the snails and the poultry stock. Bring to boil, reduce slightly and thicken it with the remainder of the butter.
Add the tomato cubes, the parsley and the finely chopped dill. Season to taste with pepper and salt.

The tabouleh
Dry the tabouleh, the French beans, paprika, carrots and the spring onions well.
Mix all ingredients well and season to taste with pepper and salt.
Before serving heat it in the steam oven or pan with olive oil.

The rabbit medallions
Cut the rabbit fillets into medallions (5 from each fillet)
Mix the thyme leaves with the peanut oil.
Season the medallions with pepper and salt and put them in the thyme-flavoured peanut oil.
Heat the grill pan until it is very hot and grill the medallions on both sides so that they show a chequered pattern. Arrange them on a baking tray and, just before serving, put them for 3 minutes in a preheated oven at 180 °C (depending on their thickness).

ARRANGEMENT ON THE PLATE

Put a strip of the tabouleh on the plate and arrange the Namur snails on it with some parsley and dill (in plumes).
Arrange the medallions alongside and pour a little sauce over them.
Finish off with the vegetable cubes.

21

Jonnie Boer
De Librije
Zwolle (NL)

The journey to Zwolle takes us through the Veluwe, an extensive stretch of unspoilt nature in the middle of the Netherlands. Here all the beauty nature has to offer bristles with life. Game, large and small, birds of all feathers, and fishes in the pools. Between the trees, wildflowers, herbs and all kinds of fungi grow. Too many to list them all.

Attention to the natural environment, the products associated with the area. That is exactly what Jonnie Boer is concerned with. The culinary extravagances in the Librije kitchen essentially involve 'down to earth' tastes. Can we say that the Veluwe has made Jonnie Boer into the master chef that he is now? In my opinion, yes. If you have enjoyed the culinary delights served by Jonnie you will be aware that he has no equal. Eating at Jonnie's is like taking a journey. Or, as Sven puts it: 'A good chef is up on a pedestal, Boer is also on that pedestal but on the tenth floor!'

Jonnie Boer is 40 ('just tell them that I am 39, that sounds younger') and is the father of a son and a daughter, Jimmie and Isabelle. He looks stern and reserved, but very quickly shows himself to be the opposite.

'Actually I wanted to go into advertising, something to do with drawing. If I was not to be found in the Veluwe when I was younger, then I was busy with my colour pencils. I was then, and still am, enormously creative. That is why I still draw at every opportunity. Every dish I design is first of all drawn out – a rough sketch – so that I can envisage in advance the best way of presenting it on the plate.'

'Sometimes I spend weeks brooding on a single detail. By drawing it, I can suddenly come up with the ideal combination. That goes for tastes as well as for the arrangement of a dish.'

'Nature is still my most important source of inspiration.'

'New techniques always attract my attention. They can offer you a new approach or a structure that gives a new excitement to an ingredient.'

Thérèse about her husband: 'Jonnie is always relaxed, wherever he is. He can get enormous enjoyment from the people around him. That is what is so typical of him: he is peace personified, even in the heat of the battle! In addition he wants – as I do – at all times to be able to enjoy our children. Our business must not be a hindrance to this. Our children are always involved whenever it is possible.'

Jonnie: 'I try to keep very peaceful in my professional life. If I get stressed about it, I only pass the stress on to my staff. We can't afford that in our way of life. My children are everything to me. As soon as the doors of the restaurant close, all my attention is focused on Jimmie and Isabelle.'

'It is an absolute priority for me to be able to place trust in my people. So I put the young apprentices doing a placement in our restaurant right next to me by the serving hatch. Only then can they learn the trade at the highest level. By giving them trust and responsibility you create independent cooks with potential!'

'Thérèse is the ideal wife for me. We complement each other. She does her work in her territory, the dining room; I do mine in the kitchen. We do that with mutual involvement. We criticize each other positively, making suggestions, and that works.'

'Music can be a huge inspirational influence'

26

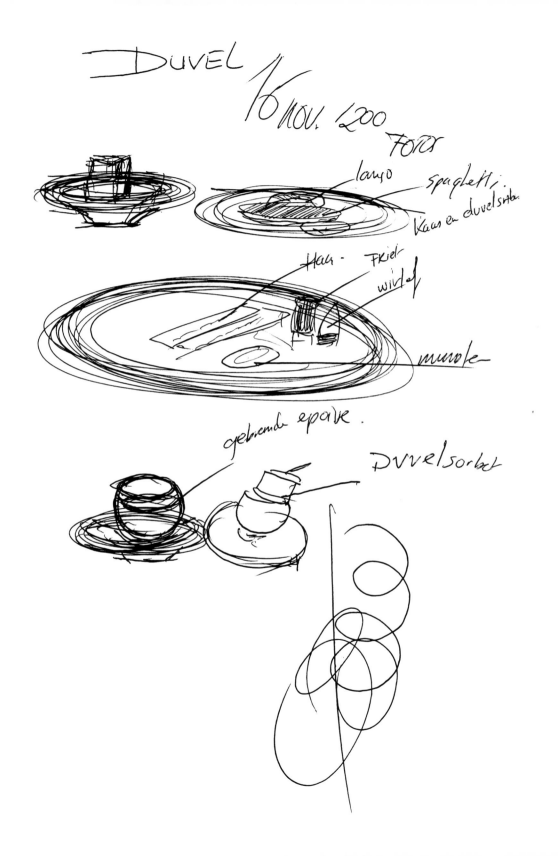

DUVEL

16 NOV. 1200

Foror

lauso   spagLetti.

Kaas en duvelsab.

Haa.   FRiel

wirtof

murole

gebrande epave.

DUVELsorbet

'I am colour blind, but that is no disadvantage to me at all. If I can't see anything clearly, I just ask. Sidney, my right-hand man, supports me perfectly in this.'

'It is very important to me to have music in the background. Music, for example, Miles Davis, can be enormously relaxing for me and at the same time it is a huge inspirational influence.'

'Before the service I am always rather nervous, but in a positive sense. It is the 'push' I need. That is why every day my wife and I have built in a private rest period between four and six. That is when we have time for ourselves and for our children. It means that I can build myself up for the time of performance without it becoming a routine.'

'I have two passions: football and motorbiking. Football is something in which I can lose myself completely. I play football every Sunday morning, and afterwards enjoy it with my son Jimmie. We are great Ajax fans.'

'Biking is a real release. Then I am completely at one with nature. Not the speed, but the enjoyment comes first. In the past I had a quotation painted on my Harley: "The harder they come, the harder they fall"!' Speaks for itself, doesn't it?

'As soon as the doors of the restaurant close all my attention is focused on Jimmie and Isabelle.'

'I have used beer a lot in my cooking and for a long time. Duvel is one of my "all time favourites". I am a great advocate of serving beer with some dishes instead of wine. You have to remember that if you use beer as an ingredient, you have to take care how much you use. A few drops may be enough to bring a dish to perfection. A few drops too many can completely ruin that same dish.'

30

Hot langoustines
with spaghetti, paprika and sabayon of Duvel
with a mature farmhouse cheese

Tartare of langoustines
with beetroot and Duvel tea

INGREDIENTS

Dish 1 :
- 1 packet of spaghetti
- 16 langoustines
- 4 piquillo paprikas
  (Spanish flambéd paprika)
- 2 egg yolks
- 10 cl Duvel
- 50 g mature cheese (mature, old cheese)

Dish 2 :
- 3 shallots
- 2 cloves garlic
- 1 large carrot
- 1/2 litre fish stock
- 2 red beetroots
- 10 cl Duvel
- 1/2 litre poultry stock
- 6 leaves of gelatine (per litre of liquid)
- juice of 1/2 lime

PREPARATION

Hot langoustines with spaghetti, paprika and sabayon of Duvel with a mature farmhouse cheese

Cook the spaghetti al dente in plenty of salted water and rinse till cool.
Select the four largest langoustine tails and fry them in the shell.
Arrange the strings of cooked spaghetti next to each other, cover with a layer of the piquillo paprikas and finish off with another layer of cooked spaghetti.
Cut out circles or squares with an Inox cutter.
Stir up a sabayon of Duvel. For this beat the egg yolks together with the Duvel over heat until light and airy. Stir in the very thinly grated cheese.
Peel the fried langoustine tails.

Tartare of langoustines with beetroot and Duvel tea

Remove the tails of the langoustines and rinse them under the tap, peel them and set the remainder aside.
Chop the heads and the shells fine and together with the chopped shallots, garlic, carrot and the fish stock use it to make a tasty consommé.
Add the Duvel last and leave it to simmer for about 10 minutes. Pass it through a fine conical strainer.
Peel the beetroots and cut them into small pieces. Pour the poultry stock over them and continue cooking until they are done.
Puree them and pass them through a fine conical strainer.
Add six leaves of gelatine per litre.
Allow the beetroot consommé to cool completely. Put the lightly gelled mixture into a piping bag and put this in the refrigerator.
Chop the langoustine tails to a fine tartare and season to taste with lime juice.

ARRANGEMENT ON THE PLATE

On one small plate place the spaghetti tartlet with the fried langoustine on top, finish with Duvel sabayon.
On the other small plate place a ring mould. Arrange the tartare in this and pipe the beetroot on it from the piping bag.
Remove the ring and dribble Duvel consommé round the dish.

Cabbage-fed hare with Münster cheese, kale and sauce royale enriched with Duvel

INGREDIENTS

- *2 full saddles of hare*
- *200 g kale*
- *20 cl water*
- *1 onion*
- *1 large carrot*
- *1 leek*
- *100 g hare blood*
- *100 g butter*
- *15 cl Duvel*
- *50 g goose liver*
- *2 shallots*
- *300 g potatoes*
- *10 g ripe Münster cheese*
- *2 cloves*

PREPARATION

Cut the fillets from the saddles and remove any membrane.
Brown the bones and the rest of the hare with pieces of carrot, the onion spiked with two cloves, and the leek in the pan. Pour on water until covered and simmer to make a stock.
Clean the kale. Put the kale with a little water in the blender and puree it until a smooth consistency is obtained.
Bring plenty of water to the boil in a pan and add the pureed kale.
Drain the kale through a cloth and keep it in a dark, cool place.
Cook the potatoes and work in the Münster cheese. Rub it though a hair sieve and if necessary season to taste.
Divide the stock in two.
Work the first part into the drained kale.
Heat the second part until it has almost come to the boil, and work in the butter and the blood. At the last moment pour in the Duvel. Do not allow it to boil after this.
Sear the fillets of hare on both sides and leave them to rest briefly.

ARRANGEMENT ON THE PLATE

Arrange the hare fillets on a plate and finish them off with the two sauces.
Serve with the Münster puree, make a dip in it and pour a little melted butter into it.

Epoisses crème brulée, fennel sorbet

INGREDIENTS

For the crème brulée :
- *35 cl milk*
- *1 Epoisses cheese of 250 g*
- *1 leaf of gelatine*
- *2 g salt*
- *3 fresh egg yolks*
- *cane sugar*

For the fennel sorbet :
- *650 g fennel juice*
- *50 g Duvel*
- *80 g grape sugar*
- *60 g glucose*
- *2 g salt*
- *2 leaves of gelatine*

Preparation

Crème brulée
Heat the milk slightly and add the Epoisses (without the crust and cut into pieces), the gelatine (soaked in water), the salt and the egg yolks. Stir well together.
Strain the mixture into dishes and place them covered in an oven at 95 °C for 30 minutes.
Leave the crème to cool.

The fennel sorbet
Warm all ingredients lightly and melt the gelatine into it. Leave to cool.
Pour into the sorbet maker and turn until a smooth mixture is obtained. (It is very difficult to make the fennel sorbet without an ice-cream maker). If you have no ice-cream maker you can put the juice in the freezer and stir it every quarter of an hour, in this way you will have a granité after a few hours.

ARRANGEMENT ON THE PLATE

Finish the crème with a brulée of cane sugar.
Serve with the fennel sorbet or granité.

36

Wout Bru
Bistrot d'Eygalières
Eygalières (F)

Eygalières, a small village somewhere between Marseilles and St Rémy de Provence. It is hard to find a more idyllic place: a few narrow lanes on a hill, a pleasant Provençal ambience, and a view that on sunny days – and there are plenty here – stretches to the snow-capped top of Galibier, a giant French peak.

The light shines impressively on the picturesque cottages. An incidence of light that has already captivated the many artists who have found it – and still find it – a great source of inspiration.

Not only painters, but also master chefs – as it appears!

One of the 'enlightened' chefs is Wout Bru, born a Belgian, but gradually becoming a true Provençal. Apart from an Antwerp streak, which is enduring.

It is now some ten years ago that Wout and his wife Suzy, also a true-born Fleming, took the plunge to begin their life's work in this special part of the world. A vacant grocery shop in the rue de la République was bought and magically transformed into a delightful bistro, with several luxury hotel rooms adjoining. Thanks to the delicious Provençal raw materials, but particularly to a large amount of culinary talent, professional knowledge and enthusiasm, the culinary fairytale gradually took on a magnificent form. So now we can say with pride: 'The little Belgian has become a true culinary giant!'

Wout Bru is 36, and has one son, Boris, and a daughter, Lou. A rather business-like and reserved first impression soon makes way for that of a striking personality.

'When we started with the bistro I was a real "ambition fiend" to my staff. The stress, the responsibilities, it almost led to a breakdown. I have now learnt to live with the pressure. I am a completely new man in that respect. A well-trained and strong team, like my staff is today, is essential for a successful business. Close relations with your staff creates mutual trust in both directions, which in turn determines motivation and eventual success at the top level.'

'Before we ended up in Eygalières, Suzy and I were real backpackers. We travelled from place to place and on the way gathered practical experience in various catering establishments. I still remember vividly how we lived in "cabanons" (small cabins) with a minimum of comforts. Those adventures hardened us and made us what we are now.'

Suzy on Wout: 'Wout always was and still is a perfectionist. Whereas he now displays a positive and dynamic attitude, in the past he was more of a fault-finder. He has now found himself and has become another man, much more relaxed. But I think that is not only the result of years of experience, but also of being a father. Since the birth of Boris, Wout has been an ideal father who spends a great deal of time with his children.
We have been together now for 17 years. A single glance between us is enough to communicate and to understand each other without many words. Wout has enormous talent. I love his cooking – and him too, in fact!'

Wout: 'I may perhaps be lazy, but only to gain the essential positive energy. I need deadlines to make me give of my best. I have learnt to shake the load off my shoulders in moments of stress. I now know that my former nervousness was a sign of weakness, of uncertainty. Nowadays if a problem crops up, I try to find a solution to it which will satisfy everybody.'

'My great source of inspiration? That is every step I take out of doors here in Eygalières. Strolling through the local markets, idle chatter, immersing myself in the local atmosphere. After that I go back to work relaxed, creating and developing in my head and on the plate.'

'I intend to collect my recipes together. Increasingly I catch myself wanting to do something about this. After all, I have been working independently for ten years now and have come to the conclusion that I have not kept a record of anything. So I hope this book will spur me on, a good resolution to keep an account of everything in the future.'

'Am I a puree person? Well yes, I have a weakness for it. I like the structure and the texture. Puree can be served very light or, on the other hand, quite firm. That can give a new 'feel' to a dish, create a different intensity.'

'I have acquired a new passion, golf!' To which Suzy reacts: 'Wout, you only played golf once and found it boring! Wouldn't you rather carry on with cross country? Cross country suits him much better. He can get rid of his aggression that way.'

'To me cross country means switching off my mind completely and going hard at it. Switching off does not mean that you don't need to concentrate. Otherwise you would soon have an accident here among the rock formations.'

'I relax on my machine. I can do my own thing and give it my all. I recently bought a quad for my son, Boris. Now we can go for short rides together. That is heaven for me!'

'DUVEL… is a real discovery for me. You should know that it is not easy to find a good quality beer here. Not to drink, let alone to cook with. At first I was in a quandary what to cook with Duvel. But what does a chef do then? Quite right, he experiments. I was really surprised by the result. It requires some research but once you have found the right proportions, you can achieve the most remarkable results with Duvel. Cooking with Duvel is a must for every lover of gastronomy.'

'I relax on my *machine*'

Raw scallops
with goose liver,
Duvel vinaigrette

INGREDIENTS

For the vinaigrette :
- *5 cl soya sauce*
- *5 cl sherry vinegar*
- *15 cl Duvel*
- *2 g salt*
- *4 g demerara sugar*
- *5 g garlic puree*
- *20 cl pine nut oil*

For the scallops :
- *5 g apple brunoise*
- *5 g pumpkin brunoise*
- *5 g avocado brunoise*
- *5 cl olive oil Chez Bru*
- *3 cl balsamic vinegar of Modena*
- *8 scallops*

For the accompaniment :
- *mixed salad of choice (e.g. green frisée)*
- *10 g julienne of black truffle*
- *4 slices white bread without crusts*
- *4 slices goose liver*
- *sea salt and freshly ground black pepper*
- *10 g julienne of Ganda ham*
- *2 leaves of gelatine*
- *8 flat Zeeland oysters*

PREPARATION

The vinaigrette
First make the vinaigrette. Put all ingredients in a blender except for the oil. Mix everything together and bind it with the pine nut oil.

The scallops
Mix the brunoises (diced fruits) with the olive oil and balsamic vinegar.
Cut the scallops into even slices (one into three).

The accompaniment
Open the flat oysters, take them out of their shells and let them drain.
Mix the salad with the truffle and season to taste.
Fry the slices of bread in the frying pan with a little olive oil.

ARRANGEMENT ON THE PLATE

Arrange the brunoise on a plate and place two Zeeland oysters and a warm slice of bread on top, put a slice of goose liver on top, seasoned with sea salt and black pepper, and distribute the julienne of Ganda ham over it.
Place the scallops on top of that.
Finish off with the mixed salad and a line of Duvel vinaigrette and balsamic vinegar.

Fritters with Duvel and petits gris snails, paprika coulis with ginger

INGREDIENTS

For the fritter batter :
- *300 g flour*
- *20 g demerara sugar*
- *3 g salt*
- *4 eggs*
- *25 cl ice cold Duvel*
- *5 g tarragon leaves, finely chopped*

For the paprika coulis :
- *2 red paprikas*
- *15 g ginger*
- *5 cl olive oil Chez Bru*
- *30 cl full cream milk*
- *10 cl Duvel*
- *sea salt and black pepper*

For the petits gris snails :
- *20 petits gris snails*
- *1 large shallot, peeled*
- *50 g extra fine French beans, cooked al dente*
- *1 large tomato*
- *2 cl sherry vinegar*
- *5 cl olive oil Chez Bru*
- *5 g tarragon leaves, finely chopped*

PREPARATION

The batter
First make the batter. Mix the flour with the sugar and salt. Stir the eggs in and beat until there are no lumps in it. Finish off with the cold Duvel. At the last minute add the tarragon. Leave to rest for half an hour.

The paprika coulis
Clean the paprika and the ginger and cut both into cubes. Braise them in olive oil. Add milk and Duvel and season to taste. Continue to cook gently for 30 minutes on a low heat. Puree and pass through a fine conical strainer.

The petits gris
Take eight petits gris and cut them in equal pieces; do the same with the shallot and the French beans. Skin the tomato and take the seeds out, cut it into even cubes. Mix with the vinegar, olive oil and tarragon leaves.
Pull the rest of the petits gris through the beer batter and deep-fry them at 180 °C until they are a golden yellow and float to the top. Drain them on a napkin.

ARRANGEMENT ON THE PLATE

Arrange the cubed mixture on a plate and put the fritters (three per person) on top of it. Finish off with a coulis of red paprika.

Perch fillet
poached in Duvel consommé

INGREDIENTS

- 20 cl poultry stock
- 20 cl Duvel
- 1 bouquet garni
  (thyme, bay leaf, parsley, 1/2 shallot)
- 4 perch fillets, 160 g each
- 500 g pumpkin
- 1/2 litre milk
- 10 cl Duvel
- 1 large tomato
- 4 leaves of basil
- 250 g 'horn of plenty' mushrooms
- 2 shallots, finely chopped
- 1 clove of garlic, chopped
- 50 g butter
- 3 cl balsamic vinegar
- pepper and salt
- 10 cl olive oil Chez Bru

PREPARATION

Make the consommé by briefly boiling the poultry stock and the Duvel with the bouquet garni (about 5 minutes).
Put the perch in the stock and poach it for about 8 minutes (depending on the size of the fillets).
Cut the pumpkin into cubes, bring them to the boil with the milk and the Duvel, simmer until done. Puree the pumpkin and season to taste with pepper and salt.
Skin the tomato and take out the seeds, cut the tomato into a brunoise. Chop the basil and mix it with the tomato.
Braise the cleaned 'horn of plenty' mushrooms together with the shallots and garlic in the butter.

ARRANGEMENT ON THE PLATE

Arrange the mushrooms on a plate and put the perch on top.
Spoon the tomato brunoise on top, then a spoonful of the Duvel consommé and a few drops of balsamic vinegar.
Finish off with the pumpkin puree.

Rudy Buchet
Au Sanglier des Ardennes
Oignies en Thiérache (B)

'A culinary outstanding and, moreover, professional succession from father to son' is how you could summarize the Buchets' history. The leading restaurant which his father, Jacky, started many years ago in picturesque Oignies en Thiérache, with its two streets and a church, has gradually been taken over by his son Rudy. Jacky is still there in the kitchen, but he now leaves the leading role to his son. The family, originally a family of butchers, has over the years built up a reputation for game. What else can you expect in the middle of hundreds of square miles of Ardennes forest? The experts say it is one of the best areas for shooting game in Europe. And the best game the sportsmen can bring home is prepared in sublime fashion in the famous restaurant, Au Sanglier des Ardennes, highly renowned by lovers of game from far and near.

Rudy Buchet is 38 years old and has three children; Jeremy, 15, is just starting his chef's training (the start of the third generation?), Grégory is 13 and Alexy, 10. Rudy is enormously hospitable and despite the great success of his business a modest man.

'As a butcher's family, we grew up with cooking from childhood. Jacky used to help in his father's business from an early age. Meanwhile my grandmother cooked meals for the seasonal workers in the district. But it quickly became clear that dad had great talent as a cook and he gradually developed into his mother's right-hand man. They started up a restaurant and like my father I was, years later, the boy who helped his parents. My brother, on the other hand, reopened the family butcher's business next door to the Sanglier, and specialized in the traditional art of Ardennes charcuterie.'

'The traditions of the game kitchen are still quite recognizable in our kitchen. And we want to keep it like that: a variety of game dishes are prepared according to the hunting seasons, casseroles, terrines… each dish has its history, which we bring up to date in harmony with modern trends. Through the years the restaurant has in this way developed its own style from which it never deviates. Of course, on appropriate occasions I produce the necessary innovations and variations.'

'I draw my inspiration from nature, which here is ubiquitous. As soon as I step outside, I am surrounded by it. I am extremely fortunate to be able to pick all kinds of mushrooms myself. You can't get them any fresher. Woodland and other fruits in season are just waiting to be picked. And on top of this there is an enormous variety of game, my treasury!'

Father Jacky about his son: 'I have a great respect for my son. Nothing is more difficult than to follow in your father's footsteps and still do things in your own way. Rudy now has complete responsibility for the kitchen, my job is just to assist him in this. He is bubbling over with creativity and in spite of all his success still remains simplicity itself.'

Rudy: 'I never actually get worked up. Of course there is stress, but I have learnt to keep that under control, it can even act as a stimulant. Two things help me in this, one rather more healthy than the other. I smoke – too much, actually – and I am passionately fond of the forest. That way I still get my healthy ration of oxygen.'

'From childhood the men in our family have had their own dogs. My dog is Chopin, a dachshund, a born hunter. When I go out beating – driving the game that will then be shot – he is my faithful companion.'

'Hunting is a collaboration between those who drive the game and those who shoot it. Driving is a skill passed down from father to son. You always do it with the same group of people. It relaxes me and keeps me in tune with nature. That is how I can shrug off the stress of the restaurant.

'From childhood the men in our family have had their own dogs.'

'We are right in the middle of Trappist country here. I am happy to put Duvel next to them. Like the Trappists, Duvel has a history and that is what I like. It is a beer full of character and individuality. Just as a wild boar has its own taste, you can't compare the taste of a Duvel with that of any other beer. It lends itself perfectly to the preparation of the best game stews.'

59

Fillet of wild duck with 'aigrelette' sauce, sauerkraut with Duvel

Casserole of wild rabbit with Duvel

INGREDIENTS

- 2 breast fillets of wild duck
- 10 cl Duvel
- 200 g sauerkraut
- 25 cl cream
- 5 g Ardennes mustard
- pepper and salt

PREPARATION

Heat the sauerkraut together with the Duvel
Brown the scored duck breasts on the fatty side first, in this way you don't need to use butter. Put them in a preheated oven until done.

The 'aigrelette' sauce

Drain the liquid off the sauerkraut and add it to the cream; leave this mixture on the heat to reduce slightly (producing a sourish, or 'aigrelette', sauce).
When it has acquired the desired thickness, add the mustard.
Season to taste with pepper and salt.

ARRANGEMENT ON THE PLATE

Carve the duck breasts into slices.
Put a small mound of sauerkraut in the middle of a heated plate.
Arrange the duck breast round it and finish off with the 'aigrelette' sauce.

INGREDIENTS

For the casserole :
- 100 g dried prunes (without stones)
- 1 wild rabbit, cut into pieces
- flour
- 100 g butter
- 5 cl olive oil
- pepper and salt
- 1 large carrot
- 10 shallots
- 1 stalk green celery
- 200 g mushrooms
  (champignons de Paris)
- 3 bottles of Duvel
- thyme, bay leaf
- 5 g strong Ardennes mustard
- 1 slice of old bread

To accompany :
- boiled potatoes

PREPARATION

Soak the prunes in water overnight.
Dust the pieces of wild rabbit with flour.
Melt the butter with the olive oil in a casserole and brown the rabbit pieces in it. Season with pepper and salt.
Remove the rabbit from the casserole and braise the cut-up pieces of vegetable (carrot, shallots, celery and mushrooms) in it.
Deglaze with the beer and add the prunes, the thyme, bay leaf and the rabbit.
Spread the slice of bread with mustard and put it mustard-side down on the contents of the casserole. Bring the contents to the boil.
Turn the heat low and leave to simmer for 1 1/2 hours.
Take out the pieces of rabbit and keep them hot.
Reduce the sauce to the desired thickness and – if necessary – season it with pepper and salt.

ARRANGEMENT ON THE PLATE

Serve in a deep plate and add some boiled potatoes.

Christian Denis

Clos St. Denis

Vliermaal (B)

'the *basic ingredient* is *sacred* to me'

Not far from Tongres, the oldest town in Belgium, is a magnificent castellated farmstead with adjoining restaurant, Clos St. Denis.

These buildings, dating from the seventeenth century, together with their sophisticated interior and splendidly laid out gardens, make an imposing impression. So does Christian Denis, two-star master chef, and his charming family. I found it a little awe-inspiring, I must admit, when I, as a young buck, had to meet such an old stager. Christian Denis is, after all, one of the godfathers who has for a long time stood at the summit of Belgian gastronomy.

On our arrival we were soon introduced to the Denis family, who are very important for Christian. Everything involves the family. All decisions are carefully considered and carried out in consultation with the whole Denis family.

Christian Denis is 57, husband to Denise, and the father of two daughters. Véronique is responsible for the restaurant's renowned patisserie, while Nathalie, together with her mother, faultlessly directs the friendly welcome and the service.

'I regard myself as a seasoned professional. I can look back on 45 years of experience and am not afraid to go against the stream of current fashions in cooking. I know what good taste is and go for seasonal products which will allow themselves to be developed into a first-rate final result.'

'Year after year I strive to achieve a constant and very high quality. That does not mean, however, that I am insensitive to trends. I only reject some techniques that in my opinion have nothing to do with gastronomy. For instance, everyone seems to follow the craze for a succession of small dishes, which have almost pushed out the aperitif appetizer. Everything has to look more and more special and spectacular, with the risk that eventually people will start experimenting with what is impossible. You then end up with restaurants competing with each other, as it were, on the basis of appetizers and delicacies with the coffee. What has that got to do with dining and taste? That is one of the things I am fighting against.'

'I was born with the spirit of Escoffier (the French master chef), with a deep respect for the product with which I go to work. The basic ingredient is sacred to me.'

'I have periods of creativity. Afterwards I start to write, draw and try things out. Sometimes it leads to something, at others it results in nothing. Or something that did not work years ago suddenly today slots together like the pieces of a jigsaw. Often it is just a subtle distinction, a few grams of an ingredient, that makes a world of difference.'

Denise, his wife, describes him: 'Christian is very strict, particularly on himself, but that is just because he is aiming for absolute perfection. When Christian shuts the kitchen door behind him, then he relaxes totally, then he lives for his family and the grandchildren.'

Christian describes himself: 'I am strict and a control freak. It is the only way to succeed and to keep going. Anyone can have a weaker moment when something can go wrong. But if it happens a second time it does not go unpunished. In our world, where achievement is a matter of course, you pay dearly for that weaker moment. I may be 57, but it is my "craft" to work for perfection every day. And yes, why not try for a third Michelin star.'

'My "collector's mania" for unique, special works of art and antiques provides my relaxation. In the past I looked mainly for majolica porcelain by Botino. Among other things, I also have an extensive collection of antique glassware. These days I mainly collect carved coconuts. There are real pearls among them. If that involves a trip to London or Paris that is an extra bonus, including the culinary delights there.
If I call it my "collection mania" that is because I buy an antique piece ever week. Sometimes they are pieces for my collection or for the restaurant, but I am also looking for plenty of furnishings for the hotel we are hoping to open soon. Collecting is in fact quite a family trait. My wife collects silver and my son-in-law, Renaud, our master sommelier, collects corkscrews.'

'In my demanding requirements for the "ideal" ingredient I have in the past experimented with various kinds and brands of beer. A few ideal beers stood out and Duvel was one of them. In addition to being a perfect beer for drinking, Duvel has the advantage of having a lot of acidity, which makes the beer technically very interesting for cooking. If you allow Duvel to reduce, all those delicious sugars surface again. The bitterness, too, is a specific property which makes Duvel unique. I compensate for it by adding butter, which results in a splendid combination.'

'I am strict and a control freak'

Supreme of goose- and duck livers
with spice cake and Vrolingen syrup,
chutney of conference pears with Duvel beer

INGREDIENTS

For the supreme :
- *150 g duck liver*
- *150 g goose liver*
- *3 g fine salt*

For pear balls :
- *3 dl red wine*
- *1 teaspoon fine granulated sugar*
- *1/2 stick of cinnamon*
- *lemon rind*
- *1 pear*
- *1 x 100 g slab of unsweetened spice cake*
- *1 g mixture of 5 peppers*
- *2 cl calvados*
- *50 g Vrolingen syrup (pear- and apple syrup)*

For the pear chutney :
- *250 g pears*
- *10 cl Duvel*
- *15 g lemon*
- *30 g sugar*
- *1/2 stick of cinnamon*
- *1/2 vanilla pod*
- *50 g roasted almonds*

PREPARATION

The supremes

With a small knife remove as much as possible of the sinews and veins from the duck and goose livers.

Mix the livers in a stainless steel bowl and season to taste with salt and the mixture of 5 ground peppers and the calvados. Pack the livers in a piece of plastic film and shape this into a sausage of about 5 cm in diameter. Close it off well at the ends and pack the whole parcel in aluminium foil. Leave the sausage to rest overnight in a refrigerator. Preheat the oven to 68 °C and cook the duck- and goose-liver sausage for 18 minutes. Take the sausage out of the oven and immediately plunge it into a bowl of iced water. Then let it rest in the refrigerator for a further 12 hours.

The pear balls

Make a sugar syrup of the red wine and the granulated sugar, the cinnamon stick and the zest of the lemon; cook scooped-out balls of pear in this.

The spice cake

Cut the spice cake into thin slices and cut out 24 circles with a 4 cm diameter cutter. Toast the slices of spice cake. Leave them to cool and spread syrup on them.

The chutney

Cut the pears into 1/2 cm cubes and put them into a pan with the other ingredients. Leave to simmer until the pears are done and the juice has been reduced completely. When the chutney has cooled, add the grilled almonds.

Take the duck- and goose-liver sausage out of its package, cut it into twenty slices (5 mm thick) and finish these off smoothly with a cutter.

Form four small turrets of 5 slices liver and 6 slices spice cake; starting with a slice of spice cake, next put a slice of liver on it, finishing off with a slice of spice cake.

ARRANGEMENT ON THE PLATE

Place the turrets of liver and spice cake on cold plates. Garnish with dried pear. Next to it place a quenelle of the Duvel chutney. Finish off with some almonds.

71

Tatin of chicory with acacia honey, fried turbot and a reduction of Duvel beer

INGREDIENTS

- 8 chicons of chicory
- 40 g clarified butter
- 4 teaspoons granulated sugar
- lemon juice
- preserved lemon rind
- 1 thin slice farmhouse bread
- peanut oil
- ground chicory
- 4 turbot fillets of about 120 g each
- 25 g clarified butter
- salt, freshly ground pepper

For the sauce :
- 1/2 bottle Duvel beer
- 2 dl chicken stock
- 50 g butter
- salt and pepper

PREPARATION

The chicory
Clean the chicory. Set aside 4 leaves for garnishing. Arrange the chicons in a buttered casserole. Season with pepper and salt and pour a cup of water over them. Allow this to simmer gently. Remove the chicory from the casserole, drain it and leave it to cool. Cut the chicons of chicory into 3 cm long pieces.
Take small stainless steel moulds with an 8 cm diameter. Melt 10 g clarified butter in each mould, add a tablespoon of granulated sugar and leave it to simmer gently on the edge of the range until a pale caramel begins to form. Next arrange the pieces of chicory in the moulds and put them in the oven for about 10 minutes until they are done.

The garnish
Cut the slice of farmhouse bread into quarters. Spread these with peanut oil, dust them with chicory powder and place them in a preheated oven for 8 minutes at a temperature of 200 °C to dry them out. Leave them to cool.
Cut the bottom half of the chicory leaves into a julienne and save the points. Mix the julienne with a few preserved lemon rinds and a few drops of lemon juice. Fill the chicory leaves with this.

Reduce the chicken stock together with the beer to half the quantity.
In a frying pan heat 25 g clarified butter and fry the seasoned turbot fillets in this.
Warm the chicory moulds in the oven.
Heat the reduction of beer and stock and bind this with 50 g butter. Season with pepper and salt.

ARRANGEMENT ON THE PLATE

Place a chicory mould in the middle of each plate, remove the circle and arrange the turbot on top of the chicory. Garnish with chicory leaves and the slices of bread. Serve the sauce separately.

73

Caramelized puff pastry with apples, sorbet of Duvel beer

INGREDIENTS

For the sorbet :
- *2 dl water*
- *200 g sugar*
- *1 bottle of Duvel beer*

For the puff pastry with apples :
- *16 rectangular slices of puff pastry of 12 x 4 cm*
- *50 g icing sugar*
- *150 g custard cream*
- *200 g cream, whipped*
- *4 apples, Jonagold*
- *25 g clarified butter*
- *25 g granulated sugar*
- *caramel sauce*

PREPARATION

The sorbet
First prepare the sorbet. Bring the water to the boil with the sugar. Allow to boil vigorously for a few minutes and then cool down. Add the bottle of beer and pour this mixture into the sorbet maker.

The puff pastry
Preheat the oven to 220 °C. Bake the rectangular slices of puff pastry between 2 baking trays until they are done and have the desired colour.
Dust them with castor sugar and caramelize them under the grill. Leave to cool.
Mix the custard cream with the whipped cream and fill a piping bag with a large round nozzle with it.
Peel the apples, cut them in half and remove the core. Cut them into 2 cm cubes and fry them in a pan in the clarified butter. Sprinkle them with fine sugar and let them caramelize gently. Leave to cool on a tray.

ARRANGEMENT ON THE PLATE

For each plate garnish 2 puff pastry biscuits with apple, arrange the cubes neatly in a row and fill up with the mixture of custard cream and whipped cream. Next put them on top of each other and on top of that put a third one, garnished only with custard cream. Finish off with a fourth biscuit to close off the pastry. Dust with castor sugar.
Place them on cold plates, garnish with caramel sauce and a spoonful of Duvel sorbet.

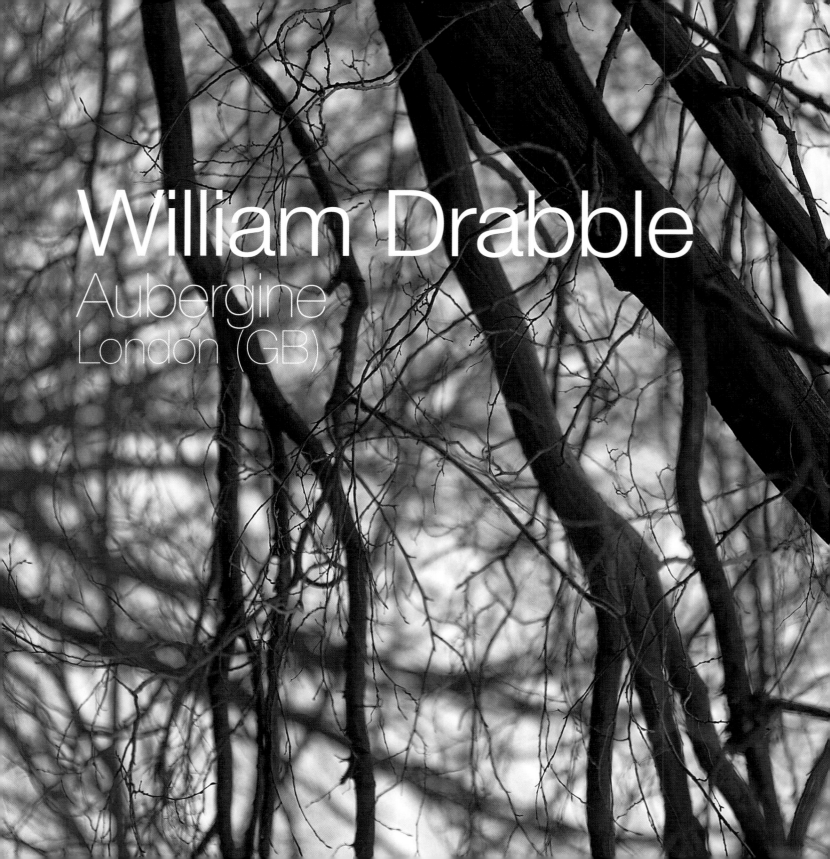

William Drabble

Aubergine
London (GB)

London is not only rich in historic buildings and culture, but also has a large number of world-renowned restaurants. One of them is the Aubergine, once put on the map by master chef Gordon Ramsey. When he left, six years ago, the young William Drabble was selected as the new chef. Although it would not be a simple matter to follow in the footsteps of such an illustrious personality and celebrated chef as Ramsey, Drabble took up the challenge… and succeeded brilliantly! So much so that the memory there of his predecessor is perhaps beginning to recede into the background a little. His abilities have also recently been rewarded by the prestigious London 'Lunch of the Year' award.

William Drabble is thirty-four and has a Flemish partner, Claudine. At first sight you would perhaps take him for a taciturn Englishman, but nothing is further from the truth. William is a jovial man, who sweeps you along with his enthusiasm for his trade.

'I gained my first Michelin star when I was twenty-five. With hindsight; that was much too early. But well, if you get a star, you don't refuse it. However, the pressure it brings with it should not be underestimated. Particularly if, as I was, you are still in a culinary development stage.'

'I spent my youth in the English countryside, surrounded by farms full of lambs, cattle and pigs. I enjoyed nothing more than hanging around the local farmers and I learnt as a child to judge a beast for appearance and taste.'

'When I was a child my grandmother ran a bed & breakfast. She also cooked for the local squire. She was a great inspiration to me as a child. To the extent even that she may have been the unconscious impetus that brought me to my present job.'

'The cardinal point for me is not the visual creation of a dish, but its pattern of tastes. So I like to keep my cuisine "simple" and I am no supporter of dishes presented in a way that is too complicated (or exaggerated). I prefer to work with about four ingredients, each of which can be brought to perfection separately. Better that than a jumble of about twelve ingredients which may perhaps produce a pretty visual effect, but result in a cacophony of tastes.'

'I try to keep peaceful and calm at all times, even though I lead a stressful life. If you are too intense and dynamic, this leads to a negative attitude among your staff, which in turn does no good to anyone. I think it is very important to work with a well-trained team. Then the whole team radiates enthusiasm and professionalism and that's how you get good results.'

Thierry Tomasin, the Aubergine's French manager, sums up William: 'He is a hard worker and yet radiates calm, which has a very infectious effect on the staff. He is the perfect 'team player' and a leader who respects his people and listens to them. The customers, too, even during the service, get his full attention. This is in fact very exceptional among

'My boyhood dream was to play football'

80

top chefs. William has in this way built up a unique bond with his customers over the years. The Aubergine's motto is: "Have fun, enjoy yourself and keep an eye on the customer". That is what people come back for. William is a true countryman at heart. He not only knows the product itself, but also how it is cultivated, its origins – in short he knows all the virtues of the products he uses.'

William: 'Once a year I take time off to visit my most important suppliers. "Being a chef" is for me not just something that happens only in the kitchen. I want to see what is going on among the farmers in their fields and barns. Empathize with the fishermen inland and at sea. I like learning about the foods I serve. I also go to the market on average twice a week to get the feel of the suppliers and the products that I work with. These experiences are a very important part of my trade.'

'Cooking depends 70 percent on the quality of the product and 30 percent on the talent and skill of the chef.'

'My boyhood dream was to play football for Liverpool, but my talent was rather too modest for that! Even now I would like to go into training and play football to keep my figure in shape. But I have a good excuse; I don't have time for it. (…or is it willpower,' he mutters under his breath).

'I let off steam by going for a walk every day with my bull mastiff Amber. In that way I can relax completely and get rid of any stress. It completely clears my head and my mind.'

'Duvel… is no stranger to me. It is Claudine's Flemish mother's favourite beer. Duvel is a splendid beer to work with in the kitchen. It offers plenty of culinary opportunities, it can upgrade the other ingredients and give them added value.
In addition to an extensive wine list, the Aubergine also has a fine list of beers, with Belgian beers playing the leading part. For some dishes we advise the customers to drink beer instead of wine.'

81

INGREDIENTS

For the belly pork :
- *1 kg piece of belly pork (on the bone)*
- *1 onion, chopped*
- *4 cloves of garlic*
- *2 carrots, sliced*
- *1 leek, chopped*
- *2 sticks of celery, chopped*
- *10 sprigs of thyme*
- *20 peppercorns*
- *pinch of salt*
- *piece of smoked bacon rind*
- *500 g clear honey*
- *2 tablespoons cracked black pepper*

For the cabbage :
- *1 cabbage*
- *100 g heavily smoked belly bacon*
- *4 tablespoons pork fat*

For the potatoes :
- *2 onions*
- *25 g butter*
- *4 large baking potatoes*
- *500 ml chicken stock (strong)*
- *1 bottle of Duvel*
- *20 g butter*
- *24 slices (20 cm long, very thin)*
  heavily smoked belly bacon

For the smoked bacon gravy :
- *300 ml good veal gravy*
- *200 ml of Duvel*
- *1 piece heavily smoked bacon rind*
- *4 sprigs of thyme*

Glazed belly of pork with cabbage, potatoes with Duvel infusion

PREPARATION

Belly pork
Place the belly pork in cold water, bring to the boil, then refresh in cold water. Put the pork in a clean pan and cover it in cold water. Bring to the boil and add onion, garlic, carrot, celery, leek, thyme, peppercorns, bacon rinds and a little salt. Cook very slowly for 2 1/2 to 3 hours until the rib will just pull out. Leave to cool in cooking liquid. When cool enough to handle, remove from liquid. Remove ribs and cartilage. Remove skin with a sharp knife (not the fat). Place the pork into a deep roasting tray, pour honey over it, sprinkle with pepper. Place it in the oven at 160 °C and baste every 5 minutes until glazed with honey and pepper. When glazed remove it from the oven and leave it to rest before slicing. Slice the meat across the grain.

Cabbage
Remove dark green outer leaves from the cabbage and discard them. Break down leaf by leaf until you get to the very yellow leaves and use the heart for something else. Select nice green leaves, remove the stalks and slice the cabbage very thinly. Remove the rind from the belly bacon and cut the bacon into lardoons of 3 x 3 mm thickness. Put pork fat in a pan and fry bacon until it starts to caramelize. Add cabbage and cook slowly until cabbage is soft (without frying). Season (but be careful: fat and bacon are already salty and pork peppery). Drain off excess fat. Just warm through in the pan when needed.

Potato wrapped in bacon
Slice 2 onions, braise slowly in butter until caramelized. Drain them, refrigerate. Peel 4 large baking potatoes. Cut them into round slices 2 mm thick, 6 cm in diameter, 8 per portion. Bring chicken stock and the Duvel to the boil. Add the potato slices. Poach until three-quarters cooked. Remove from stock and spread out on a tray to cool. Season the potatoes. Make stacks of two slices each. Place some caramelized onion on the top of each stack of two. Stack to a height of 8 slices of potato and onion. Wrap potato stacks in smoked bacon. Where ends of bacon meet, skewer with a cocktail stick. Place wrapped potatoes into a pan, pour boiling chicken stock over it. Add butter. Cover in tin foil and place in a pre-heated oven at 180 °C for 15-20 minutes. Leave to rest for 5 minutes. Remove potatoes from stock. Reduce stock to glaze. Glaze potato with the reduced stock.

Smoked bacon gravy
Take veal gravy and Duvel, bring to the boil, add thyme and bacon rind.
Infuse until gravy tastes of thyme and smoked bacon.

ARRANGEMENT ON THE PLATE

Put the cabbage in the centre of the plate. Place glazed potatoes in the centre on top of the cabbage. Stack belly pork on top of the potato. Poor a little gravy around the outside of the cabbage.

INGREDIENTS

For the escabeche :
- *1 onion, sliced*
- *2 carrots, sliced*
- *12 cloves of garlic, sliced*
- *25 saffron strands*
- *400 ml white wine vinegar*
- *400 ml olive oil*
- *salt*
- *cayenne*
- *1 teaspoon crushed coriander seeds*
- *1/2 bunch coriander, tied*
- *50 ml Duvel*
- *20 picked coriander leaves*

For the coriander oil :
- *100 g coriander*
- *100 ml vegetable or peanut oil*
- *salt*

For the croûtes :
- *12 slices crusty bread*
- *1 clove of garlic cut in half*
- *1 teaspoon olive oil*

For the fennel salad :
- *1 small bulb of fennel*
- *a little frisée lettuce*

For the mullet :
- *8 fillets from 12 oz red mullet,*
  pin-boned and trimmed
- *2 tablespoons olive oil*
- *salt*
- *lemon juice*

Mullet escabeche with Duvel

PREPARATION

For the escabeche
Heat 100 ml of the olive oil gently. Add the sliced carrots, onion and garlic. Season with a little salt and cayenne pepper. Add crushed coriander seed wrapped in muslin. Cook slowly, without colouring, until soft. Add white wine vinegar, saffron and the fresh, tied coriander. Boil rapidly until vinegar is reduced. When vinegar has gone, add remaining 300 ml oil. Bring to the boil, cook slowly for 5 minutes. Add 50 ml of Duvel. Bring to the boil, and season to taste. Leave to cool. When cool remove the coriander seeds and fresh coriander.

For the coriander oil
Plunge 100 g of fresh coriander into boiling salted water. Bring back to the boil, boil for 30 seconds. Pour into a sieve, push out any excess water. Put coriander into a liquidizer with 100 ml of vegetable oil and liquidize well. Pour into a muslin cloth with a bowl underneath to catch the oil. Squeeze out oil. Leave to settle, skim oil off the top and set aside in the refrigerator.

For the croûtes
Take some nice crusty bread rolls and slice them 5 mm thick Rub an oven-proof tray with a clove of garlic and a little olive oil. Put the croûtes on the tray and bake at 160 °C until golden brown. When golden, remove them from the oven and put the croûtes on kitchen paper.

For the fennel salad
Slice the fennel as thinly as possible across the fibres. Put the slices on a tray and sprinkle with a little salt. Leave for half an hour. Wash fennel in ice-cold water, drain onto kitchen paper. Mix fennel with a little frisée lettuce and dress with a little escabeche oil and salt.

To cook the fish
Gently heat a large Teflon frying pan and add oil. Add seasoned red mullet fillets, skin side down, and cook gently. When two-thirds cooked, flip over fillets and remove pan from heat (the residual heat will finish the cooking). Season with a little lemon juice.

ARRANGEMENT ON THE PLATE

Warm the escabeche of Duvel and add a few of the picked coriander leaves.
Place 1 tablespoon of escabeche in the centre of each plate.
Place 3 croûtes on top Criss-cross mullet fillets on top of that.
Drizzle a little coriander oil around.
Finish off with the salad on top.

85

Peter Goossens
Hof van Cleve
Kruishoutem (B)

Obviously Peter Goossens was very high on the list of chefs we absolutely had to have working with us on this project. In the space of only a few years time Peter has breathed new life into Belgian gastronomy. That is clear from the number of customers who flock to Kruishoutem, even from abroad, to sample Peter's exquisite cuisine. So it was only to be expected that in 2005 Peter should receive his well-earned third star.

'It all starts with the
main ingredient'

Kruishoutem, close to the line where the Belgian Ardennes begin: a farming village, a village green by the church, surrounded by some houses and fields. Somewhere among all this is a small but splendidly renovated farmhouse, the former property of a farming family called Van Cleve. It now houses a unique Belgian three-star restaurant, and number one in the Belgian Gault Milliau. Through the windows of the restaurant you look out on the rolling countryside of the Flemish Ardennes, with all the region's changeable character. A sunny landscape that in an instant changes into a dreary and dismal nothingness. Inside you are wrapped in a pleasant ambience, supported by a sense of style. Several paintings by the local artist Roger Raveel animatedly underline the landscape, some full of colour, others pale and sober.

Peter Goossens is 40 years old and the father of three children, Bernard, Virginie and Arno. His wife, Lieve, controls the dining room team with a light hand and plenty of flexibility. Peter, on the other hand, is the Sphinx. He supervises the kitchen where he is a man of few words. Peter aims for perfection in the organization and you sense that as soon as you put a foot in his territory. His staff understand what he means without many words.

'I have my own way of working, have created my own system and I keep to it. My cooking is done along the lines I set down. I call them my own 'sacred five'. It all starts with the main ingredient, you look at it, decide on the aroma, the taste. Then the 'cuisson' is decided, the preparation. Frying, grilling, poaching, steaming… The next step is the choice of garnish. That is perhaps the most difficult link in the chain. Its accompaniments can push a basic ingredient right into the background or distort the taste. And that is certainly not the intention. The same risk lurks in step four, the sauce. Fifth and last comes the presentation. Many chefs make the mistake of putting presentation in the forefront, with unfortunate consequences for their final result.'

'The dishes are first created in my head and only later do I write them down, try them out and test them. At the moment I am completely tied up in a period of experimentation with different structures, especially in the area of temperatures: ice cold, cold, warm, hot. Then there is the idea of giving added value to an ingredient by an element of acidity. This is where I can, for example, enormously appreciate a beer such as Duvel, particularly for its bitterness.'

'The excitement, but also the stress, of our profession is that every day we have to sit two tests, the midday service and the evening one. We can't allow ourselves any bad patches. That is why I attach the greatest importance to the continual support and motivation of my staff and you can't do that if you wield the sceptre like a despot. For instance, I think it is extremely important to be with my kitchen brigade every day. I like to eat with my staff at lunchtime. It emphasizes the solidarity and team spirit which in turn leads to a better collaboration!'

As soon as the doors of the restaurant close, it is the turn of the children and a circle of friends. The friends are in fact people from a world not concerned with catering. Deliberately so. 'I try to avoid being constantly confronted with my professional life. I don't want to be smothered in professionalism.'

Lieve, his wife, describes him: 'Peter is extremely dedicated, but he never forgets how far he should go or what his limitations are. Only in his leisure time does he succeed in setting aside his compulsion.'

Peter describes himself: 'I know what I want and where I want to go. My object is quality and seeking the perfect balance between taste and presentation. I don't want to fall back into a vicious circle, but to innovate and achieve. But always with the idea of keeping both my feet on the ground.'

Peter seeks quality in his passions too. These also affect his presence and his emotions. 'Passions take shape from a culture, your origins.'
To the question of how he should best be presented outside his kitchen he doesn't have to think long for an answer. 'We'll go and smoke a cigar in Antwerp, in Mike's Havana House!'

'I am a confirmed smoker, that is to say, of cigars. No, not those little thin ones, but a big, robust cigar. For me smoking a good cigar is pure relaxation, it soothes me and lets me recharge my batteries after the stress of work. For me a cigar is culture, it gives me a certain status. A status which I want to keep up in my life as a chef, but also as a human being.'

92

'Belgium has an abundance of good beers. Among them Duvel is for me one of the best. Its pronounced bitterness, the miracle of the second fermentation, these are only some of the factors that make Duvel a better ingredient to serve as a basis for a selection of dishes. Magnificent sauces, casseroles, or combined with fresh or smoked varieties of fish. Actually, it should be a challenge for every chef to get to work with an ingredient like Duvel. Some ten years back I was already experimenting with beers, and now it frequently happens that a dish flavoured with beer appears on the Hof van Cleve menu, and that beer is served with it, too.'

Fried sole with oxheart cabbage and mussels, Duvel sabayon

INGREDIENTS

For the sauce :
- *2 shallots*
- *sprigs of thyme*
- *bay leaf*
- *nut of butter to braise*
- *50 g heads of prawns*
- *1 dl water*
- *1 dl Duvel*
- *50 g butter*

For the sole :
- *4 soles, approx. 500 g each*
- *flour*

For the mousseline :
- *100 g potatoes, peeled*
- *25 g cold butter*
- *2 to 3 cl warm milk*

For the oxheart cabbage :
- *1 oxheart cabbage*
- *30 g butter*
- *60 g mussels, cooked*
- *chervil*
- *butter for frying*
- *pepper, salt and nutmeg*

PREPARATION

The sauce
Peel the shallots, chop them into small pieces and braise them together with some thyme and bay leaf in the butter. Add the prawn heads and fry them briefly with the shallots. Add the water and Duvel and bring the mixture to the boil. Allow to infuse for 30 minutes. Strain the sauce. When the rest of the dish is prepared, bring 1 decilitre to the boil and mix in the butter. Season to taste with pepper and salt.

The sole
Ask the fishmonger to prepare the soles ready for cooking. Wash the soles and make sure there are no traces of blood left. Pat the fish dry, season them with pepper and salt and dust them lightly with flour. Next fry them until pale brown. The sole is cooked when the fillets separate slightly from the bone at the head. Remove the bones and bring the soles back into shape. Keep them warm.

The mousseline
Cook the potatoes until done (preferably steamed). Puree the potatoes. Mix the cold butter with the puree. When the butter has been absorbed completely, add the milk. Mix the milk through the puree with a beater. Heat, if necessary, while stirring with the beater. Season to taste with pepper and nutmeg.

The oxheart cabbage
Cut the oxheart cabbage into quarters. Remove the hard core and cut the leaves into thin strips. Cook in salted water until done. Cool it straight away in ice-cold water to retain the colour. Melt some butter and briefly braise the cabbage. Season to taste with pepper and salt.

The mussels
Heat the mussels in a little of their own cooking stock.

ARRANGEMENT ON THE PLATE

Put the two bottom fillets of the sole on a plate. Place the oxheart cabbage in the middle and put the top fillets on them. Arrange the mousseline on top of this. Garnish with the mussels and the chervil. Beat the sauce in a mixer until it foams and pour a little foam round the fish. The rest of the sauce is served separately.

95

Casserole of pig's cheek with Duvel and croquettes of sweetcorn

INGREDIENTS

For the pig's cheek :
- *150 g onions*
- *2 bay leaves*
- *2 sprigs of thyme*
- *butter for frying*
- *1 kg pig's cheeks, cleaned*
- *black pepper and salt*
- *300 g brown stock*
- *1 bottle of Duvel*
- *beurre manié*

For the croquettes :
- *1 tin of corn (850 ml)*
- *75 g Parmesan cheese, grated*
- *6 leaves of gelatine per litre
  of strained corn*
- *egg whites for coating*
- *panko (Chinese breadcrumbs) for coating*

PREPARATION

The pig's cheeks
Slice the onion finely and braise it in the butter, together with the bay leaves and thyme. Season the pig's cheeks with pepper and salt and sear them in lightly browned butter. Add the pig's cheeks to the braised onions.
Pour the brown stock and the Duvel over the pig's cheeks and bring it all to the boil. Continue the cooking process in a preheated oven at 220 °C. Take the cooked cheeks from the oven and keep them hot. Strain the sauce and reduce it a little to taste. Bind the sauce with some 'Beurre manié' (a well-kneaded mixture of equal quantities of butter – at room temperature – and flour). Season to taste with pepper and salt.

The croquettes
Chop the corn finely together with the grated Parmesan cheese. Rub the mixture through a sieve and discard the skins. Season to taste with black pepper and mix in the molten gelatine. Pour the mixture into a rectangular mould and leave to set in the refrigerator for a few hours. Next cut the set mixture into rectangles. Pull the rectangles first through egg white and then panko. Deep-fry them until they are a golden yellow.

ARRANGEMENT ON THE PLATE

Arrange the pig's cheeks next to each other and pour a little Duvel sauce over them. The rest of the sauce is served separately.
Arrange the corn croquettes parallel to the pig's cheeks.

Salad of prawns, avocado and Duvel sorbet

INGREDIENTS

For the sorbet :
- *1 dl water*
- *50 g sugar*
- *1 bottle of Duvel*
- *5 drops of lemon juice*
- *1 g stabilizer*

For the tomato and avocado :
- *1 tomato*
- *1 avocado*
- *1 tablespoon extra virgin olive oil*
- *1 lime*
- *4 slices of brown bread without crusts*
- *200 g Ostend (or Dutch) prawns, hand-peeled*
- *pepper and salt*

PREPARATION

The sorbet
Bring the water to the boil with the sugar. Add the Duvel, the lemon juice and the stabilizer. Leave to cool and then turn in the ice-cream maker.

The tomato
Peel the tomato and remove the seeds. Cut the fruit into cubes. Deep-fry the peel of the tomato until it is crisp.

The avocado
Peel the avocado, remove the stone and cut the fruit into cubes. Combine these with the tomato cubes, olive oil and a few drops of lime juice. Season to taste with pepper.

ARRANGEMENT ON THE PLATE

Serve the avocado and tomato mixture in an attractive glass. Cover it with a small slice of brown bread. Put the prawns loosely on top and garnish with a ball of sorbet and the deep-fried peel of the tomato.

Sergio Herman

Oud Sluis

Sluis (NL)

In the distance tosses the tempestuous North Sea, and rather closer we hear the gentle lapping of the Eastern Scheldt. Should I perhaps describe Sergio Herman in the same way?

Sven and I arrive in the peaceful, still sleepy, little town of Sluis just before our host. While Sven is setting up his equipment to photograph the dishes, a trendy off-road vehicle stops in the Oude Beestenmarkt. A nervous individual gets out of it. My first impression is to recognize the shadow of a young Nick Cave.

Sergio has something about him of the rock star arriving at the theatre where a few hours later he will give the performance of his life.

And that is in fact what happens. A quick coffee, and then he starts straight away. Few words are exchanged between Sergio and his staff. A look, a single word, here apparently everything happens automatically. Across this apparently austere pattern the base tones of modern grunge and other turbulent rock sounds boom in the background. During the service silence, the same automatic activities, and Sergio reigns! The customers come in, their orders are passed on to the kitchen and Sergio goes to work, just like the tossing of the tempestuous North Sea.

Sergio Hermans is 34 and has one son, Boy. He looks like someone who will always go to extremes, and that is indeed the case. 'While the cooking goes on I am hyper-concentrated. I want to have everything under control all the time. In our small kitchen brigade everyone is tuned to everyone else so that it all runs like a well-oiled machine...'

'Actually, I never wanted to be a chef, but fate decided otherwise.'

'My cuisine is one of tastes and combinations of taste. I go on looking until I have found a unified whole, and then I build on that. I don't just put a sprig of dill to finish off a dish unless there is a good reason for it. If I do something like that it is because I have thought about it. Everything must be in keeping with the end result with all the ingredients in balance. Only when everything is right am I satisfied and only then is a dish fit to go on the Oud Sluis menu.'

'For me presentation is the last stage in the development of the dish. These days I use almost only white plates. That makes my dishes stand out when they are served.'

'I am particularly keen on creating fish dishes and desserts. Among the ingredients that are important to me are garlic, lemon and olive oil. The last only from Spain, pressed from Arbequina olives.'

'I always want to hear music. I have no preference for particular genres or styles. Classical today, rock tomorrow. Listening to music relaxes me. It helps me, stimulates me. To create and innovate is my principal consideration, a necessity even. If I had to prepare the same dishes year in year out, then I would rather stop.'

104

His mother describes him: 'Sergio is a distinctive character, at one moment completely peaceful, the next up in arms. He is often uncertain: am I really doing all I can? He can put in enormous effort. I sometimes have the feeling that he is too self-effacing.'

Sergio describes himself: 'I can really work my fingers to the bone. I am certainly no artist, I do my job. But I still always like to spring a surprise. However, I am a real Zeelander, which means that I have both feet on the ground. I don't see anything wrong in that, I know my limitations.'

'Walking along the beach, that is a wonderful source of inspiration too. For me the sea air is a drug; everything in my head starts to work like a radar. That is when the ideas start to come. Ideas which I can then get to work on in the kitchen.'

'Several times a year I go with my wife, Nancy, who has her own hairdressing salon near Bruges, on a trip to the city.
We enjoy ourselves, relax, eat well at the establishments of colleagues and visit several museums, because I like art. I can get enormous enjoyment from a fine work of art. Its structure, its subject, its colour palette. On the other hand, I am no artist myself, you can't call cookery an art.'

'I enjoy a good glass of beer, and certainly a Duvel. Cooking with Duvel is a challenge. Its bitterness plays an important role in it. The balance of the final result can be destroyed by a centilitre too much. So you must work out carefully how you use Duvel and how to incorporate it in the right proportions. Once you get the right result, you can achieve staggering combinations of taste.'

'Actually, I *never* wanted to be a chef'

Grilled turbot with fried Zeeland lobster, cream of Jerusalem artichokes and lobster sauce with Duvel and spices

INGREDIENTS

For the lobsters and the turbot :
- 2 Zeeland lobsters each of 500 g
- court bouillon
- 1 clove garlic
- 4 sprigs of thyme
- 4 pieces of turbot each of 125 g

For the Jerusalem artichokes :
- 250 g artichokes
- 1/2 dl cream
- 1/2 dl milk
- 1 1/2 dl poultry stock

For the oxheart cabbage :
- 4 leaves of oxheart cabbage
- 100 g salted butter

For the lobster sauce :
- 3 dl lobster liquid
- teaspoon ground spices (star anise, coriander seed, mace and cardamom)
- cream
- 4 tablespoons Duvel beer
- pepper and salt
- 1 dl olive oil

PREPARATION

The lobsters
Cook the lobsters in the court bouillon, leave them to cool and cut them in half. Season them with pepper, rub them with garlic and sprinkle with thyme. Dribble olive oil over the lobsters.

The turbot
Grill the turbot and season with pepper and salt.

The artichokes
Peel the artichokes and cock them in the cream, milk and stock until done. Drain them and puree them.

The oxheart cabbage
Blanch the oxheart cabbage and braise it in butter with pepper and salt. Roll the leaves up thinly.

The lobsters and lobster sauce
Fry the lobsters in olive oil and add the butter. Leave to stew gently and briefly. Reduce the lobster stock slowly to half the quantity and season with the lobster gravy from frying, the spices and a little cream, add Duvel at the last moment and stir. Poach the oysters in their own liquid with the champagne and a knob of butter.

ARRANGEMENT ON THE PLATE

Draw a nice line of artichoke cream on the plate, arrange the turbot next to it and place the lobster on top; finish off with the oxheart cabbage and draw lines of sauce round it.

Three coffee structures,
with a sabayon of chocolate
and Duvel

INGREDIENTS

For the sabayon :
- *4 egg yolks*
- *75 g sugar*
- *1 dl Duvel beer*
- *30 g cocoa*
- *2 dl cream*

For the granité :
- *25 cl coffee*
- *25 g sugar*
- *5 cl amaretto*
- *5 cl Kahlua*

For the dough :
- *6 egg whites*
- *200 g butter*
- *200 g sugar*
- *100 g flour*

For the ice cream :
- *35 cl milk*
- *15 cl coffee*
- *100 g egg yolks*
- *165 g sugar*
- *50 cl cream*

For the cream :
- *250 g mascarpone*
- *12.5 cl cream*
- *1 espresso*
- *1 leaf of gelatine*
- *a dash of grappa*
- *a dash of Tia Maria*

PREPARATION

The sabayon
Beat the egg yolks, sugar and beer until the mixture is cold.
Then fold the whipped cream into the mixture.

The granité
Mix all ingredients and place in a low tray in the freezer.
Stir occasionally.

The dough
Melt the butter and mix in the other ingredients. Stir well.
Leave to rest overnight.
Spread the mixture onto silicon mats and bake. Shape into cylinders.

The ice cream
Beat the egg yolks and sugar to a white consistency (ruban). Let the milk and coffee infuse and pour it on the ruban. Allow to thicken (but do not allow it to boil) and add the cream.
Leave to freeze overnight.
Turn it the following day.

The cream
Heat the espresso and dissolve the gelatine in it.
Pour the cream onto the mascarpone and blend carefully.
Fold in the cream and bring to taste with the grappa and Tia Maria .

ARRANGEMENT ON THE PLATE

Fill the cylinders with granité and mascarpone cream and dust them with cocoa.
Draw a line with the sabayon and put the ice cream next to it.

Eddy Kerkhofs
Il Piccolino
Los Angeles (USA)

The greatest stars of this planet mostly live in or near Los Angeles, 'city of a thousand stars'. This city needs more than a few words for an introduction: apart from LA there are also Beverly Hills, Santa Barbara, and of course, the ever worldly and celebrated Hollywood, to say nothing of the attractive beaches. So an interesting place for a young chef to put down roots and build up a culinary temple from scratch? Well, it's been done by a Belgian. His name? Eddy Kerkhofs.

A good 25 years ago Eddy Kerkhofs ventured to renovate a building on Sunset Boulevard. This boulevard, in the 1920s still one of the most famous streets on the west coast of America, had half a century later fallen into decay. Eddy was one of the pioneers who took on the revival of Sunset Boulevard's famous past. In a very short while his restaurant, Le Dôme, grew into one of the hot spots of Los Angeles. Many celebrities, such as Ronald Reagan, Barbara Streisand, Richard Gere, and many others, enjoyed eating there regularly. Until in late 2004 Eddy drew a line under the story. Less than six months later he was back with a new culinary hit, Il Piccolino.

Eddy Kerkhofs is 58 and his life partner is Britt, a Swedish stewardess. If you look at the photos of his early years on American soil, he has something of the look of a real film star. Ready to jump onto the set beside Ali McGraw or Farah Fawcett, to shine in a real Hollywood hit. Could it be that he actually came to Los Angeles with the secret ambition, not to be a chef, but to be an unforgettable star of the silver screen?

'I was raised on a large farm in the Riemst area of Limburg. I got my 'culinary gene' from my aunt, who every day cooked for all the workers on the farm. Several of her recipes have always stayed with me and still today form an important basis for my cooking.'

'After studying in Namur and Brussels I ended up in Boston on the East Coast to do my final work placement. I am in fact still doing that. Only now I am the teacher and not the student, and I work for myself.'

'I wanted to come to Los Angeles, cost what it may. The world-famous stars, the magnificent city, were an enormous magnet for me. There was only one problem, I had no money. And that was just what I needed to start up Le Dôme. But if you are not rich, you have to be smart. I had the great good fortune to know several celebrities personally, and proposed a deal to them. Each lent me about $3,000, in return for which they received a post-dated cheque for $4,000 which they could spend in the restaurant. In this way I killed two birds with one stone: I raised enough cash to be able to open Le Dôme and in addition, right from the start, the restaurant was full of the most famous residents of Hollywood and its surroundings. I could not have wished for better publicity.'

'I am very strict, but extremely correct at the professional level. I always demand their best from my staff, because that is what I ask of myself. My colleagues are like an extended family. In that way you create a tie which will not break even under the greatest stress. If we sometimes have words, then I insist that any differences are talked out after the service. In that way we can start every day with a clean slate.'

'Britt and I have no children. Their place is taken by our dogs, Loebas and Mammamia. The boxers are our best friends and always keep us company. They are in fact the eighth couple of dogs we have owned. Like their predecessors they come from the Los Angeles dog's home. It is our way of contributing a little to the 'dog rescue' programme which introduces neglected dogs back into society.'

'I used to be a keen football player; Rod Stewart was one of our team. Because that is now rather too much for me, I have switched over to squash. No need to think, just play the ball.'

'Now that I have sold Le Dôme, I can enjoy life to the full. My wife and I enjoy inviting friends home and often enjoy amusing culinary moments in doing so. My private wine cellar, too, which I have built up over the years, is pure pleasure. Add a little music by Pink Floyd, the Rolling Stones, U2, Miles Davis or typically American Big Band music, and my day is made. This stage in my life is the ideal break for me, because this summer I am starting with my new culinary project: Il Piccolino.'

'But if you are not *rich*, you have to be *smart*'

'I have known Duvel for years! I have worked with it in the kitchen for a long time, and it has been greatly appreciated by my customers. Here on the West Coast I feel I am a true ambassador for Belgian beers. The recipes I have prepared for this book are real Le Dôme classics. One of them, the 'Shoulder of lamb with Duvel', I had from my aunt. Duvel is for me synonymous with my Belgian roots. In short, a beer with balls!'

117

Shoulder of lamb
à la Tante Marie,
or Shoulder of lamb with Duvel
RECIPE DATING FROM 1920

INGREDIENTS

- 4 onions
- 4 large carrots
- 8 cloves of garlic
- 200 g butter
- 10 cl olive oil
- 1 large shoulder of lamb,
  cut into 2 cm pieces
- 4 large potatoes, peeled
  and cut into slices
- 8 tomatoes, skinned and cut into quarters
- 1 bouquet garni (thyme, bay leaf, parsley,
  rosemary, chervil)
- 3 litres Duvel
- pepper and salt
- cornflour

PREPARATION

Clean and slice the onions, do the same with the carrots
Crush the garlic cloves, remove the skins and cut them finely.
Melt the butter and the olive oil and brown the pieces of shoulder of lamb in them.
Cover them with the onions, potatoes, carrots, tomatoes and the bouquet garni.
Pour all the Duvel over this and bring to the boil
Cover the pan and put in an oven at 160 °C for about 90 minutes until done.
Season to taste with pepper and salt. Before serving it can be bound – if desired – with a little cornflour and water.

ARRANGEMENT ON THE PLATE

Serve the various ingredients on a single plate, the potato, carrot, onion and tomato and the meat.
Finish off with the sauce and a sprig of green, for instance, rosemary.

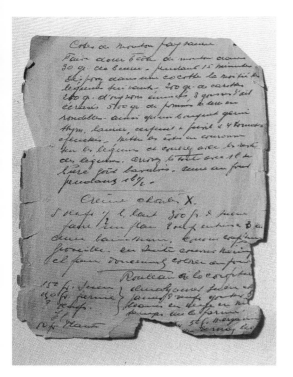

Three times crab
with Duvel sauce

INGREDIENTS

For the crab :
- *3 kinds of crab to choice*
  (king crab, snow crab,
  Californian sea crab)
- *3 carrots*
- *3 oignons*
- *1 blanched celery*
- *crushed pepper corns*
- *40 g salt*

For the Duvel sauce :
- *500 g basic mayonnaise*
  (2 egg yolks, 5 g mustard,
  pepper and salt, 1/2 litre peanut oil)
- *10 g horseradish puree*
- *10 g hot mustard*
- *3 ml Worcester sauce*
- *10 cl Duvel*
- *pepper and salt*

PREPARATION

Court-bouillon
Wash and clean the carrots, onions and blanched celery and cut them into large
pieces.
Together with the crushes peppercorns and the salt, put them into a pan with 3 litres of
water and boil for 30 minutes.
Cook the crab in the court-bouillon.

Mix the mayonnaise with the other ingredients.

ARRANGEMENT ON THE PLATE

Serve the Duvel sauce with the three kinds of crab.

Manuel Martinez
Le Relais Louis XIII
Paris (F)

Paris, City of Light! La merveilleuse!
Disappointingly, not many people seem anxious
to smile in this great, wonderful city. Its inhabitants
give a rather surly impression. And as a foreign
visitor you may consider it a small miracle if you
survive the Parisian traffic without a scratch!
Fortunately we have an excellent guide. Chef
Martinez is a Spanish Basque by origin, but one
who was born and bred near Calais, in Blériot
Plage – so almost in Flanders.
And Martinez can't conceal that he has some
Flemish blood in his veins: he is hospitable, big-
hearted and is an eloquent talker.
I begin to feel at home in Paris!

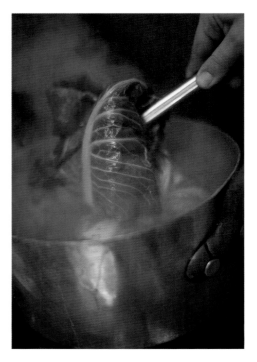

Le Relais Louis XIII restaurant is in St-Germain des Prés. Its façade hides stirring tales from an illustrious past. If only its walls could speak. It was in this house – which now accommodates the restaurant – that the Dauphin who became Louis XIII was proclaimed the new king of France after the murder of his father, Henry VI. More recently Picasso came to dine here daily during his Paris period. The studio where he painted Guernica, among other things, is just next door to the restaurant.

Manuel Martinez is 52 and the father of two daughters: Marine and Magali, who look after the reception in the restaurant.

'Cooking was my first great love. I grew up with cooking from childhood. My grandmother had a kind of eating house in the mining district of northern France. There at a young age I got to know the traditional cuisine of casseroles, civets, ragouts, pot au feu and, of course, all kinds of terrines. Now these dishes are still my most important source of inspiration.'

'What starts as a traditional pot au feu, on another day forms the basis of an overwhelmingly tasty terrine. You pull the meat into thin strips, mix it with the vegetables and pour the gelatinous gravy over it – and enjoy…'

'Over the years I have trained myself. Determined my own direction. In 1986 I was awarded the title Meilleur Ouvrier de France (a prestigious title in French gastronomy) and I have two Michelin stars – do I have to be put on a pedestal for that?'

'All those chefs who these days practice more chemistry than cooking… they are mad and don't understand what it is all about. Where are we heading, what has happened to the individual character of taste?

'Learn to know your products, learn to appreciate them in their simplicity and their taste. I have spent nearly 40 years in the kitchen and three times a week I go to Rungis (the gigantic wholesale market just outside Paris where you can find anything to do with eating) where I personally select my products.

Fresh products are the most important source of my inspiration. My trip round Rungis is always the same. I start with the fish, then the meat, poultry and 'abats' ('innards' and processed meats). Then I buy my vegetables and fruit to finish up in the hall where dairy products are sold.'

'Where will you still find a piece of meat that was hung on the bone for some two to three weeks? That is one of my rules. That is how you create real tastes.'

'If you want to conjure up haute couture on the plate without any kind of organization and without a well-oiled team, then you are lost. You can't keep it up either physically or mentally.'

Magali, Manuel's eldest daughter, describes him: 'Papa has a strong character, he is very strict in his job, but at the same time he is a lovely and honourable man.'

Frank, the maître d'hôtel, describes him: 'The customer is king and if necessary everything turns on that. Manuel can treat his staff to a pithy remark, but we have great respect for him!'

Manuel describes himself: 'I do my work, I continue to drive myself. I know what I am and on no condition will I depart from it! I may be a chef, but that does not mean that I am working at my job day and night. I have a wife, Véronique, and two daughters. We enjoy life together and you have to keep that up. If not, you would go to pieces!'

'My youngest daughter, Marine, at the age of thirteen, is my greatest critic. She already has a perfect sense of taste. She has talent. Her judgments are usually right, and that is a lot at her age. For example, she says: "No papa, I won't eat there, in that restaurant the dishes are too dull. This dish is not cooked properly and is much too salt".'

'With all the bother of paperwork and standards you have to comply with, love for the job needs to be enormously important. Anyone starting with the idea of getting rich quick is in the wrong job. It guarantees failure, even if you start on a financially sound basis. You have to be constantly investing in yourself, your staff and your qualities. You can't succeed in finding your individual style in a single year. For that you need years of blood, sweat and tears.'

'From an early age I developed a great love for horses. And I have owned my own racing stable since I was 21. My passion has grown into a proper *poulinière* (a stud farm) in which I invest much of my spare time. I now have two horses running in trotting races. For me horses are not just a relaxation. They have become a drug. More than a passion, a necessity. Horse racing needs no mental effort. For me it creates an oasis of peace.'

'*Duvel is the only beer we serve in Le Relais Louis XIII. I value its taste and the fermentation which offers an enormous number of opportunities in cooking. Both as an ingredient and as a drink to accompany it. We French are conservative, but we have to admit that a beer such as Duvel, with its distinct character, will always go down well!*'

128

'For me horses are a *passion* a *necessity*'

Fried turbot,
poultry gravy with Duvel foam

INGREDIENTS

- *200 g butter*
- *10 cl peanut oil*
- *4 fillets of turbot, each 300 g*
- *1 bottle of Duvel*
- *10 cl poultry stock*
- *salt on a base of black pepper*
- *fresh thyme*

For the accompaniment :
- *2 onions*
- *12 green asparagus*
- *1 cos lettuce*
- *2 small tomatoes*
- *coarse sea salt*
- *fresh thyme*

PREPARATION

The turbot
Melt the butter in the peanut oil and fry the turbot fillets in it.
Add 3/4 of the Duvel together with the poultry stock and a few sprigs of thyme.
Put the turbot fillets in a preheated oven at 180 °C for 15 minutes.

The accompaniment
Cut the onions into thin slices and deep-fry them. Drain them on a kitchen towel.
Poach the green asparagus, the tomatoes and the cos lettuce in plenty of boiling water.
Plunge them in ice-cold water.
Distribute the vegetables on a baking tray, season them with the salt and thyme, and
put them together with the deep-fried onion slices for about 3 minutes in the oven.

The Duvel foam
Take the turbot out of the oven and drain the gravy off through a fine conical sieve.
Season the gravy (if desired bind it with a little cold butter).
Mix in the rest of the Duvel until the mixture foams.

ARRANGEMENT ON THE PLATE

Arrange the various vegetables on top of the turbot and garnish with a sprig of thyme.
Distribute the Duvel gravy round the turbot and finish off with a little Duvel foam.

Oxtail with black truffle and Duvel

INGREDIENTS

For the oxtail :
- *8 pieces of oxtail*
- *1 large carrot*
- *2 onions*
- *1 leek*
- *fresh thyme*
- *2 sticks blanched celery*
- *coarse sea salt and pepper*
- *1 bottle of Duvel*

For the sauce :
- *200 g whipped cream*
- *200 g butter*

For the accompaniment :
- *1 black truffle*
- *200 g broad beans*
- *200 g garden peas*

PREPARATION

The oxtail
Put the oxtail pieces in a pan together with the cleaned carrot, onion and leek. Add the fresh thyme and the sticks of blanched celery. Season with pepper and salt and add the Duvel. Add water until all ingredients are covered.
Bring to the boil and leave to simmer on a low heat for about six hours.
Take the meat off the bones and put it in a dish. Add the gravy and leave overnight in the refrigerator.

The sauce
Finish off the remainder of the cooking liquid with the cream and the butter. Blend the sauce – just before serving – until light and airy.

The accompaniment
Poach the broad beans and the peas al dente.

ARRANGEMENT ON THE PLATE

Put the gelled oxtail on a plate, arrange the black truffle and strips of carrot round it and the poached broad beans and peas alongside it.
Finish off with the warm and foaming sauce.

Jacques & Laurent Pourcel

Le Jardin des Sens
Montpellier (F)

The south of France, the town of Montpellier in Languedoc. Perhaps 'living like a god in France' is true here. The climate is always mild, the view imposing and, most important of all, here is a culinary paradise, Le Jardin des Sens. A piquant detail is that this restaurant is run by identical twin brothers, Laurent and Jacques Pourcel. The brothers have been at the top of the culinary world since the turn of the century. They not only reap great success on their own territory, but leave traces of it all over the world. They are currently taking part in sixteen projects, spread over three continents. Recently they celebrated the prestigious opening of W'Sens (see elsewhere) in London, and in addition have plenty of new concepts in the pipeline.

'It is the urge for challenges, the positioning of new concepts, which continually leads us on to fresh projects. It is like an addiction, to keep going in a new culinary direction.'

Two brothers, four hands to one oar. Identical to look at, complementary in their profession. Jacques is the adventurer, the entrepreneur, a bachelor, a great talker. Laurent is rather more quiet, a family man, who keeps the reins firmly in his hands in the home front at Montpellier.

Laurent is 40 and the father of Thomas, 14, and Mathilde, aged 2 1/2. He is rather reserved, but as soon as he begins to talk about his two great passions – the Mediterranean and cooking – he develops into a real ambassador of Mediterranean cuisine.

'I knew nothing of the trade until at the age of sixteen I decided to leave school and go on a chef's training course. From childhood we always ate well at home, with an eye for quality products. Mother made a culinary feast of every meal. That is probably what inspired me to move into the culinary world.'

'My cuisine is one which is constantly developing. I do what I feel like, regardless of what other people say. My brother and I attach great importance to innovation, but it is all based on Mediterranean cuisine. We are so lucky to be surrounded by the Mediterranean sea and the countries on its shores, bursting with delicious things, available fresh and full of taste. So we make grateful use of them here. There are oysters, sea urchins and countless other delicious shellfish and different kinds of fish. Freshly picked lemons, garlic, thyme, tomatoes and olive oil. Everything is at hand to be able to serve the perfect meal.'

Jacques on Laurent: 'My brother is a man of few words. He communicates by looking at you. Le Jardin des Sens is his natural environment. Laurent is as much at home in it as a fish in water, with a staff of twenty-five.'

Laurent: 'I try not to belie my origins. Neither in my appearance nor in my cuisine. I am calm by nature and will not get upset quickly. I am quite aware that we have to be constantly performing and that there is enormous pressure. We have 100 per cent confidence in the quality of our staff. Placing this trust in them is in our opinion the basis of our success.'

Jacques, of course, is also 40, but unmarried and a complete extrovert. He is jovial and likes to talk. He is the globetrotter of the two.

'I can't sit still, or I soon get bored. I want to explore new horizons, particularly in the culinary field. It fascinates me immensely to know what people are doing on other continents. What tastes, aromas and ingredients are most important to them and how they deal with them. These discoveries allow Laurent and me to start developing new projects.'

'I like to be free, of everything and everyone, across frontiers. That is why I don't own a car or a house of my own. If you were suddenly to propose that I set off for, say, Hong Kong, I could be ready in half an hour.'

'Even if you don't always find me in the kitchen, I am a chef in heart and soul. In each of our restaurants I am in the kitchen as often as possible, discovering new products with the local chefs and experimenting with tastes and aromas.'

Laurent on Jacques: 'My brother is a communicator. He makes contact very quickly and has a good understanding of human nature. This faculty is very important to us, as we employ a large number of people who are responsible for our reputation when we are not there.'

141

Jacques describes himself: 'I attach enormous importance to good human relations and like to be able to respect people who I know also respect me.'

'It was actually Laurent who dragged me into the chef's trade. He started it in order to get out of school. I couldn't do anything without him so I had to follow him after a while.'

'The Mediterranean is like a family to which I have to keep returning, 'the eyrie'. The life, the origins of the Pourcels, derives from it. What we are is largely shaped by it. I come back to it to recover and to think things out. Laurent and I have so often had conversations there which were the source of exceptional ideas and important innovations.'

Laure de Carrière, responsible for public relations, gives her views on both brothers: 'Laurent is the most reserved and shy of the two. A man of few words and many deeds. The kitchen staff is his life. Jacques, on the other hand, is extrovert, open-minded, and bubbling with new ideas and discoveries. Actually both complement each other perfectly. Neither can do anything without the other. If Jacques is visiting one of the restaurants abroad, they phone each other ten times a day.'

'It is the *urge* for *challenges*

'Duvel is a real discovery for us. After all, France is essentially a wine country, so that cooking with beer is less common here. And unknown makes unloved. We hardly dare say it aloud, but Duvel is just like a good wine. Experimenting with it has brought us some excellent results. Duvel itself requires one accompaniment and that is butter. With the two together, you have the basis to achieve numerous culinary highlights.'

143

Stuffed fillet of rabbit, preserved rabbit legs with Duvel and sweet onion, Duvel emulsion

INGREDIENTS

For the stuffed fillets of rabbit :
- *2 slices of ham*
- *30 g butter*
- *4 juniper berries, crushed and chopped*
- *50 g breadcrumb, soaked in Duvel, cut up and seasoned with pepper and salt*
- *20 g cream (40%)*
- *2 rabbit fillets, with membranes removed*
- *sea salt and pepper, freshly ground*

For the preserved legs :
- *3 cl olive oil*
- *30 g butter*
- *30 g soft brown sugar or cane sugar*
- *4 rabbit legs*
- *sea salt and pepper, freshly ground*
- *2 sweet onions (from the Cévennes), cut into rings*
- *1 dash of ground cinnamon*
- *2 bay leaves*
- *25 cl Duvel*
- *25 cl poultry stock*
- *2 apples (golden rennet), peeled and cut into cubes*

For the emulsion :
- *10 cl Duvel*
- *a pinch of demerara sugar*
- *30 g butter*
- *1 tablespoon whipped cream (40%)*

For the garnish :
- *sprigs of sorrel and ruccola*

PREPARATION

The stuffed rabbit fillet

First make the filling. Cut the ham into cubes, braise these in butter and add the juniper berries, the soaked bread and the cream. Leave to stew briefly until it has turned into a thick mixture.

Cut the rabbit fillets 'en envelope' (cutting into them lengthwise and rolling them out until they are flat) and put a layer of filling on them. Roll them up and secure them with the aid of cooking foil.

Steam for 8 minutes and leave to cool.

Before serving, remove the cooking foil, carve into slices of the desired thickness and put into an oven at 120 °C for 10 minutes until done.

The preserved legs

Heat the olive oil with the butter and the sugar. Allow the seasoned legs to caramelize in this. Remove them from the pan and put them aside.

In the same pan, braise the onion rings together with the cinnamon and the bay leaves. Put the rabbit legs on top and add the Duvel and the poultry stock. Leave to stew for 35 minutes on a low heat. Add the apple cubes and continue to stew for another 10 minutes.

The beer emulsion

Bring the Duvel to the boil and reduce for 3 minutes. Add the demerara sugar and the butter. Just before serving add the cream.

Make an emulsion with a hand blender.

ARRANGEMENT ON THE PLATE

Serve a leg and a meat roll together with the two sauces on a plate.
Garnish with sprigs of green and if desired fried rabbit cutlets.

Jacques & Laurent Pourcel

Christophe Langrée

W'Sens
London (GB)

Right in the fashionable centre of London, close to Piccadilly Circus and Trafalgar Square, in a large town house, is the Pourcel twins' newest restaurant: W'Sens. W stands for 'Waterloo' and 'Sens' is a reference to Le Jardin des Sens. The concept is further proof that the twins, Jacques and Laurent, not only have a great talent for cookery, but are also born entrepreneurs. W'Sens, opened in late 2004, can now be added to their prestigious list of restaurants. Here you will not only enjoy sublime French cuisine, but the splendid interior design will also gratify your senses.

The chef at W'Sens is Christophe Langrée, a Frenchman.
This 39-year-old Breton is no novice. In St Malo, where he
was born, he ran until recently the leading restaurant Le
Benetin, awarded a Michelin star in 1995. He took up a new
challenge when in early 2004 he was asked by the Pourcels to be responsible for the culinary leadership of W'Sens.
A task which he takes to heart with the necessary French
charm and flair, which does not go unremarked in fashionable London. The restaurant has only recently opened its
doors and can already boast plenty of positive reviews and
fully booked tables.

150

Braised cod fillet,
potato ragout, bouchot mussels
and Duvel

INGREDIENTS

For the ragout :
- 2 large potatoes
- 2 large tomatoes
- 2 kg bouchots (French mussels)
- 15 cl Duvel
- olive oil

For the cod :
- 4 portions cod fillet, each 160 g
- olive oil
- butter
- pepper and salt
- fresh basil

PREPARATION

The ragout
Peel the potatoes and cut them into cubes. Cook them 'al dente' in plenty of water.
Skin the tomatoes and remove the seeds. Cut them into cubes.
Wash the mussels, put them in a pan and pour in the beer.
Cook until the mussels open (6 minutes).
Take the flesh out of the shells and keep the cooking liquid.
Bring the liquid to the boil with the potatoes and take the pan from the heat.
Add the mussels and the tomatoes and season with pepper and salt. Finish off with a dash of olive oil.

The cod
Brown the cod in butter and olive oil and cook until done in a preheated oven at 160 °C for 8 minutes.
Season to taste with pepper and salt.

ARRANGEMENT ON THE PLATE

Serve the cod fillet on a bed of mussel and Duvel ragout.
Garnish with basil cut into strips.

153

Casserole of pig's cheeks with Duvel

INGREDIENTS

For the casserole :
- *1 large carrot*
- *1 large onion*
- *1 stick of celery*
- *800 g pig's cheeks*
- *1 bouquet garni (thyme, bay leaf, parsley)*
- *2 bottles of Duvel*
- *butter*

For the accompaniment :
- *5 cooking apples*
- *1 stick of cinnamon*
- *four-spice mix*
- *2 large potatoes*
- *6 slices bacon*

PREPARATION

The casserole
Chop the carrot, onion and celery into large pieces and put them together with the pig's cheeks and the bouquet garni in the Duvel. Allow to marinate for 24 hours.
Drain the pig's cheeks and brown them in butter.
Add the strained marinade to this and leave it to reduce on a low heat until the cheeks are soft.

The accompaniment
Stew the apples with the cinnamon stick and the four-spice mix.
Cut the potato into very thin slices.
Put each slice of bacon between two slices of potato and bake this in a preheated oven at 150 °C until they are golden brown.

ARRANGEMENT ON THE PLATE

Arrange the apple compote alongside the casserole of pig's cheeks and finish off with the crisp slices of bacon and potato.

The author, Stefaan Daeninck, is chef-proprietor of the creative culinary bureau 'Culinair Ateljee' in Tielt, Belgium. This business, in close dialogue with its customers, develops a variety of culinary products in exciting recipes, ideas and themed dishes. It provides a successful promotion of ingredients and methods of preparation, and functions as a partner in culinary demonstrations and workshops. It also keeps a sharp eye on trends within the culinary sector. Stefaan Daenincks has already published two books: 'Broodje Gezond', and 'Oesterboek Zilt, zinnenprikkelend en Zeeuws'.
info: www.culinair-ateljee.be

The photographer Sven Everaert has worked with cameras from childhood. Since then his quest for the best pictures has only widened: his hobby has developed into his career. As a freelance photographer from Ghent he has meanwhile explored the furthest limits of his inborn talent, covering all possible subjects and all continents.
His richly varied and ever-expanding portfolio includes promotional and culinary photography, portraits, design and travellers' tales. He recently opened his own studio in Ghent, specializing in culinary photography, for which Stefaan of Culinair Ateljee acts as culinary stylist.
info: www.sveneveraert.com

ACKNOWLEDGEMENTS

First of all my thanks go to all the chefs who have made time to write for me, and to all at Duvel Moortgat for their valued commission.
To Petra (my muse and literary support, with her cornucopia of words), Ferran, Jordi and … (expected in June 2005), my children and the spice of my life.
Sven and his sugarplums, his Eveline, Ava and Ella.
Johan of Ziezo, for his magnificent layout, giving full value to the text and Sven's magnificent photographs.

www.lannoo.com

Lannoo Publishers
Kasteelstraat 97 – B-8700 Tielt
lannoo@lannoo.be
Postbus 1080 – NL-7230 AB Warnsveld
boeken@lannoo.nl

recipes:

Jonnie Boer, Wout Bru, Rudy Buchet, Christian Denis, William Drabble, Peter Goossens, Sergio Herman, Eddy Kerkhofs, Manuel Martinez, Jacques & Laurent Pourcel, Christophe Langrée, Pierre Wynants

texts: Stefaan Daeninck & Petra Lambrechts
English translation: Alastair and Cora Weir
photography: Sven Everaert
concept & design: Johan Vandebosch www.ziezo.be

© Lannoo Publishers, Tielt, 2005
Printed and bound by Proost, Turnhout, 2005
D/2005/45/214 - ISBN 90 209 6123 3 - NUR 447